Following God

How to develop a Quiet time

A FORTY-DAY JOURNEY

Following God

How to develop a Quiet time

A FORTY-DAY JOURNEY

EDDIE RASNAKE

Advancing the Ministries of the Gospel
AMG Publishers
God's Word to you is our highest calling.

Following God

HOW TO DEVELOP A QUIET TIME

First Printing, 2004

ISBN: 0-89957-261-8

Edited by Karen L. Brunson and Rick Steele
Interior Layout by Rick Steele
Cover design by Daryl Phillips at ImageWright Marketing and Design, Chattanooga, TN

Printed in Canada
09 08 07 06 05 04 –T– 6 5 4 3 2 1

This book is dedicated to

Earl Chute and Gary Wyatt

At significant points in my early Christian life
these men invited me into their own times with
God and helped my quiet times with God
become a relationship instead of a ritual. I am
grateful for the investments both made in my
walk with the Lord.

Acknowledgments

I am ever grateful to my dear friends, Wayne Barber and Rick Shepherd, with whom I partnered in the conception of this Bible study series that became Following God. A big "thank you" to the folks at AMG Publishers for their high view of the Word of God and their commitment to quality, accuracy, and depth in all the Bible study resources they produce. I am grateful to partner with a publisher that places the ministry side of writing as more important than the business side. Special kudos to Rick Steele, Karen Brunson, Trevor Overcash, Dale Anderson, and Dan Penwell for their help and support. A VERY special thanks as well to my daughter, Lauren, whose proofreading and suggestions made the product so much better and whose heart for God encourages and blesses me. Most of all, I remain grateful to the Lord Jesus, who saved a wretch like me and continues to lead me in what it means to follow Him with a whole heart.

 EDDIE RASNAKE

About the Author

Eddie Rasnake met Christ in 1976 as a freshman in college. He graduated with honors from East Tennessee State University in 1980. He and his wife, Michele, served for nearly seven years on the staff of Campus Crusade for Christ. Their first assignment was the University of Virginia, and while there they also started a Campus Crusade ministry at James Madison University. Eddie then served four years as campus director of the Campus Crusade ministry at the University of Tennessee. In 1989, Eddie left Campus Crusade to join Wayne Barber at Woodland Park Baptist Church as the Associate Pastor of Discipleship and Training. He has been ministering in Eastern Europe in the role of equipping local believers for more than a decade and has published materials in Albanian, German, Greek, Italian, Romanian, and Russian. Eddie serves on the boards of directors of the Center for Christian Leadership in Tirana, Albania, and the Bible Training Center in Eleuthera, Bahamas. He also serves as chaplain for the Chattanooga Lookouts (Cincinnati Reds AA affiliate) baseball team. Eddie and his wife Michele live in Chattanooga, Tennessee with their four children.

About the Following God Series

Three authors and fellow ministers, Wayne Barber, Eddie Rasnake, and Rick Shepherd, teamed up in 1998 to write a character-based Bible study for AMG Publishers. Their collaboration developed into the title, *Life Principles from the Old Testament*. Since 1998 these same authors and AMG Publishers have produced five more character-based studies—each consisting of twelve lessons geared around a five-day study of a particular Bible personality. More studies of this type are in the works. In 2001, AMG Publishers launched a different Following God category called the Following God™ Discipleship Series. The titles introduced in the Discipleship Series are among the first Following God™ studies to be published in a topically-based format (rather than Bible character-based). However, the interactive study format that readers have come to love remains constant with each new Following God™ release. As new titles and categories are being planned, our focus remains the same: to provide excellent Bible study materials that point people to God's Word in ways that allow them to apply truths to their own lives. More information on this groundbreaking series can be found on the following web page:

www.amgpublishers.com

Preface

One of the greatest joys and comforts in my life is my time spent with God. What an awesome privilege it is to meet with Him every day, to come confidently into His presence. We cannot fully appreciate this opportunity without understanding how things used to be. Under the Old Covenant that governed Israel, only the High Priest was allowed into the Holy of Holies, and then, only one time a year on *Yom Kippur*—the "Day of Atonement." He entered in fear and trembling, knowing that if his heart was not right and his sacrifice not acceptable he would die in the presence of a holy God. A rope was secured to his ankle for such a possibility, for if he were struck dead by the Lord, no one else could go in and retrieve him. The nation would stand in silence as he sprinkled the sacrificial blood on the mercy seat. All would cheer when he came out alive, seeing that as the proof that the sacrifice was accepted and their sins were atoned for until the next year.

Yet in Hebrews 10:19–22 we read,

> *Therefore, brethren, since we have confidence to enter the holy place by the blood of Jesus, by a new and living way which He inaugurated for us through the veil, that is, His flesh, and since we have a great priest over the house of God, let us draw near with a sincere heart in full assurance of faith, having our hearts sprinkled clean from an evil conscience and our bodies washed with pure water.*

When Jesus died on the cross, the veil of the Temple which hid the mercy seat and the presence of God was torn in two from top to bottom. The presence of God was now open to all believers. We need not approach Him in fear and trembling, for our hearts are sprinkled clean and our bodies washed. The application is strong and unambiguous: "LET US DRAW NEAR!"

This book was created to be a resource to help people grow in the adventure that time with God was meant to be. My prayer is that you will find it helpful.

Eddie Rasnake

EDDIE RASNAKE

Table of Contents

THE PRINCIPLE OF PURSUIT

The prophet Isaiah wrote, *"Seek the Lord while He may be found; Call upon Him while He is near"* (Isaiah 55:6). Jehovah told Jeremiah, *"You will seek Me and find Me when you search for Me with all your heart"* (Jeremiah 29:13). Amos, another messenger from God wrote, *"Seek the Lord that you may live"* (Amos 5:6). The creation is invited to seek their Creator—and yet. . . .

Have you ever reflected on why people in general do not pursue their maker? For years I did not seek Him at all because I did not believe in Him. And yet, once I did believe, that did not change everything. As a new Christian, I pursued God passionately. I so wanted to know the One who had saved me. I had discovered a great treasure chest, and I delighted in digging as deeply as I could to revel in all that was there. Yet I have not always remained so passionate about pursuing Him. Somewhere along the way I found other things to pursue. As I dug through the treasure chest, I became distracted by some of the trinkets and lost sight of the treasure. I found service and it became a substitute for satisfaction with Him—ministry replaced majesty; work became my focus instead of worship. As I dug through the depths of this treasure, I discovered truth and became enamored by it. Knowledge about Him sidetracked me from knowing Him. Information became an end in itself instead of a means to

> "You will seek Me and find Me when you search for Me with all your heart."
>
> —Jehovah
> Jeremiah 29:13

an end. Oh, I still believed in God, but things about God practically became more important to me than God Himself. It is to my own shame that I admit I wasted years not pursuing Him who alone is worthy of our passion. I sometimes had a "quiet time" because I knew that was what a good Christian was supposed to do, but I lost sight of why. Personal devotions became just another work instead of a way to know my maker.

In recent years, God has reminded me of why I pursue Him. As I have rediscovered the missing jewel of worship, I confess, I have found delight in Him all over again. I don't know if my own experience qualifies as a secret to the pursuit of God. So many times, we see books that proclaim themselves as the next best kept "secret" to this or that. But I am not sure that anything you will read in the pages ahead will hit you like a news flash. Rather, it will serve as a refresher for some of you of what you already know, or perhaps it will provide a renewal of your focus. Remember that this forty-day study covers ground that many have trod ahead of us. The paths to God are well worn. I invite you to follow along on the journey. We begin this week with the principle of pursuit. Those who seek God will find Him, and seek we must.

Pursuit **DAY 1**

NEW EVERY MORNING

Imagine you have just met that perfect someone. That person is everything you have been looking for in a relationship. As you get to know that person, your love for him or her grows and you begin to see yourself spending the rest of your life with them. What would you do to develop a good relationship with that special someone? Would you say, "Boy, it sure was good meeting you—I hope we see each other once in a while"? Probably not. If you were faced with such a relationship, you would not likely be so passive. You would not want time with that person to be simply left to chance. Instead, you would seek that person out. You would want to spend time with that person, getting to know him or her better. You would want to just enjoy being with that special someone, fellowshipping, making him or her a priority. You would share with this person your deepest thoughts, wishes, desires and everything going on in your life. Placing extreme importance on every word he or she has to say, you would want to communicate with and listen to that person—making sure you had time together. In short, you would pursue a relationship with that person. The things that we do to get to know someone are the same kinds of things we should do to get to know God. Look back over this paragraph and think about what we discussed from the vantage point of a relationship with God. They answer the "how" of pursuing God. But there is even more of a fundamental question that must be answered first—Why?

No one would need to be asked why he or she would accept an invitation to meet with the President of the United States. If the commander in chief were going to devote some time to you, <u>you would not refuse the opportunity.</u> You would rearrange your schedule, say "no" to other commitments, make any sacrifice necessary, and you would take advantage of the opportunity. The prospect is too significant to pass up. But Jehovah is far greater than any political power or presidential office. We have been invited into the presence of the greatest person of all time. Perhaps it is the fact that the opportunity is always there that keeps us from taking advantage of it as we should. For me, one of the supreme motivations is being reminded of the greatness of God. He is more worthy of my time and attention than anything else. Time with Him satisfies the deepest needs and longings of my heart, and at the same time, makes me long for more.

Just as a wedding ceremony isn't all there is to being married, becoming a Christian isn't all there is to a relationship with God. It is only the beginning. To grow closer to God we must spend time with Him. We must follow Him. Every believer is a disciple of Jesus Christ. The word "disciple" means "follower." Every Christian is either a good disciple (follower) or a bad one, but every true believer is a disciple. What one's goal ought to be is to keep growing in being a faithful follower, developing a more intimate relationship with God as a branch does with the vine. In John 15:7–8 we see that the foundation of being a disciple is that we abide in Him and His words abide in us. It is what the saints of old often called a "quiet time" or "personal devotions"—spending time with God, listening to what He has to say, and talking with Him honestly from our hearts.

Time with God should involve Bible study—and we certainly should study the Scriptures—but Bible study cannot be merely an intellectual pursuit of information. It should be the foundation of relationship. As we read and study the Word of God, we must at the same time be pursuing the God of the Word.

Take a moment to read the following verses in their context

> *This I recall to mind, therefore I have hope. The Lord's lovingkindnesses indeed never cease, for they are new every morning; great is Thy faithfulness.* (Lamentations 3:21–22)

What an encouragement to know that God's steadfast, loyal, covenant-keeping love toward us never ceases nor fails! And yet it is so easy to go through the day and never once remember God's great love for us. We can easily get caught up and entangled in the affairs of everyday life and rob ourselves of this great source of hope.

It has been said that man can live three months without food, three days without water, and three minutes without air, but hardly three seconds without hope. It is hanging on to our hope in God that gives us the moral courage to obey His will and resist temptation. Unless we are *"looking for the blessed hope"* (Titus 2:13) of future glory, we are easy prey to discouragement and aimlessness. It takes making a choice of *"this I recall to mind,"* and the result is hope.

Perhaps the greatest truth held here is found in verse 23 in the little phrase *"they are new every morning."* I remember reading this little nugget one particular morning and being suddenly gripped with its sober reality. If the Lord's loving kindnesses and compassions are new every morning and I let other commitments and choices squeeze out time with God on a given day, then that is a part of God that I will never see this side of heaven—a missed opportunity for growth, encouragement, hope, grasping more fully the greatness of God's love.

We will spend eternity getting to know God, yet because of His love, He has made Himself known in a new way every day. But the choice is left with us. When we choose to meet with Him, we find Him. "Great is Thy faithfulness"!

Time with God satisfies the deepest needs and longings of my heart, and at the same time, makes me long for more.

" 'The Lord is my portion,' says my soul, 'Therefore I have hope in Him.' The Lord is good to those who wait for Him, to the person who seeks Him."

—the prophet Jeremiah
Lamentations 3:24–25

FOR ME TO FOLLOW GOD

THE CONSIDERATION: Based upon what I read today, what is the main point of action for me?

_To commit to spending time with God
to resolve to find a specific time
and be consistent._

THE CHOICE: Jeremiah made a conscious choice to call to mind the steadfast love of God, even in the midst of his very difficult circumstances (or perhaps because of them). Take some time to call to mind the love God has for you.

_Healing through personal issues
Kingdom
Work he has provided for us._

> "In the morning I will order my prayer to Thee and eagerly watch."
>
> —King David
> Psalm 5:3

THE COMMITMENT: Any deepening love relationship requires spending time together, and a relationship with God is no different. David wrote _"in the morning I will order my prayer to Thee and eagerly watch"_ (Psalm 5:3). Prayerfully consider this commitment to God, and formalize it by signing your name.

"LORD, I COMMIT TO FAITHFULLY SPEND TIME WITH YOU EVERY DAY FOR THE NEXT FORTY DAYS, AND TO MEET WITH YOU WITH A WHOLE HEART. I ASK YOU TO SPEAK TO ME WHAT I NEED TO HEAR, AND TO CONVICT ME OF ANYTHING IN MY HEART AND LIFE THAT WOULD HINDER ME WALKING WITH YOU."

SIGNED _Karen Campbell_

One of the best ways to know what to pray is to pray the prayers we see recorded in Scripture. Each day in our forty-day journey we will include a scriptural prayer for you to pray for yourself and others.

O God, You are my God; I shall seek You earnestly; My soul thirsts for You, my flesh yearns for You, In a dry and weary land where there is no water. Thus I have seen You in the sanctuary, To see Your power and Your glory. Because Your lovingkindness is better than life, My lips will praise You. So I will bless You as long as I live; I will lift up my hands in Your name. (Psalm 63:1–4)

Adri – Janet –
Michelle – Robin –

Main Point to Remember from Day One:
Each day God reveals something new of His love for us, and we don't want to miss it.

GROWING IN KNOWING GOD

In Philippians chapter 3, the apostle Paul writes, *"I count all things to be loss in view of the surpassing value of knowing Christ Jesus my Lord, for whom I have suffered the loss of all things, and count them but rubbish so that I may gain Christ"* (Philippians 3:8). He goes on to express his life goal as *". . . that I may know Him and the power of His resurrection and the fellowship of His sufferings, being conformed to His death; in order that I may attain to the resurrection from the dead"* (Philippians 3:10–11). Paul had come to recognize that the most important relationship in life is with our Lord. Growing to a deeper intimacy with Him made every other pursuit "rubbish" in comparison. An ever-deepening of Him, Paul recognized, was the goal of life, yet it was a continual pursuit, not a destination reached. He was not satisfied with a casual acquaintance with God. The more he knew the Lord, the more deeply he wanted to know Him. He continues, *"Not that I have already obtained it or have already become perfect, but I press on so that I may lay hold of that for which also I was laid hold of by Christ Jesus. Brethren, I do not regard myself as having laid hold of it yet; but one thing I do: forgetting what lies behind and reaching forward to what lies ahead, I press on toward the goal for the prize of the upward call of God in Christ Jesus"* (Philippians 3:8–14). The amazing thing about this statement is that it was made some twenty-five or thirty years after Paul had first met Jesus on that Damascus road. He wanted to continue growing in knowing the One who had changed his life.

Paul writes in Colossians,

> *We have not ceased to pray for you and to ask that you may be filled with the knowledge of His will in all spiritual wisdom and understanding, so that you may walk in a manner worthy of the Lord to please Him in all respects, bearing fruit in every good work and increasing in the knowledge of God.* (Colossians 1:9–10)

What does it take to walk in a manner worthy of the Lord? We are never really worthy in the sense of deserving God's grace and blessing, but that is not the point here. The focus of the word *"worthy"* is on our lives being "pleasing" to the Lord. The Greek word that is translated "worthy" here has the idea of balancing a set of scales where what is placed on one side is balanced by something of equal weight that rests on the other side. Our lives need to be lived in reflection of the worth of the Lord. We see this reiterated in the statement, *"to please Him in all respects."* Walking worthy doesn't mean we now deserve God's favor due to any "good behavior" on our part, but rather, it means our ambition should be to live our lives in a manner con-

> **"The fear of the LORD is the beginning of wisdom, and the knowledge of the Holy One is understanding."**
>
> **—King Solomon Proverbs 9:10**

sistent with what God deserves from us. As a response of gratitude for His forgiveness, mercy, and blessing, we should seek to live in such a way that He is pleased with us. But what does such a life look like?

Paul describes walking worthy with two main characteristics. First, walking worthy means bearing fruit in every good work. This points to Christian service. If we walk worthy, we seek to serve the Lord, not just ourselves. There is an "others focus" to our lives. Our pursuit of Him moves us to want to do the things that please Him. Second, walking worthy means we are *"increasing in the knowledge of God."* Simply put, we're getting to know Him better; our relationship with Him is growing. Christianity separates itself from every other religion in that its pursuit isn't linked to moral character, but to a personal relationship with our Creator. Our call is to attain more than just factual knowledge about God; we are to "know" God. The wording implies intimacy.

So how do we live all of this out? Verse 9 gives the secret. In order to walk worthy, to please God, to bear fruit, to grow in knowing Him, we must discern God's will and obey it as a way of life. We are to be "filled" with the knowledge of His will. We are to always want to know what God wants us to do. But "the walk" doesn't stop there. The *"spiritual wisdom"* spoken of tells us we are to live consistent with God's will. The Old Testament idea of wisdom went way beyond mere intellectualism. It carried the sense of applying the knowledge of God's will to life's situations. To walk worthy we must be seeking, finding and doing the will of God, and we will do that if we are developing our relationship with Him and studying His Word.

FOR ME TO FOLLOW GOD

Write down the main aspect that personally spoke to you from today's lesson.

Christianity is about personal relationship (with Christ) other religions are about moral character.

- bearing fruit
- increasing in the knowledge of God.

How do we talk to the Lord? There is much talk about prayer today, but that does not mean there is much true prayer. Prayer is talking with God. Because God knows your heart, mere religious diatribes do not constitute genuine prayer. Real prayer is when our spirit connects with the Spirit of God. It is possible to bow your head, close your eyes, fold your hands, and speak many words without ever truly praying. If you are not really speaking with God from your heart, your prayers may never go beyond the ceiling. There is a danger in group-prayer of speaking to each other without speaking to God. A similar danger exists in individual prayer if we speak religiously the words we think we ought to say instead of genuinely talking with God. Real prayer is simple conversation with God, and He is not so concerned with the words we say but rather, with the attitude of our hearts. When we talk with God, what should we speak about? I have always found the **ACTS** acrostic as a good guide for prayer. In this system, the letters "A-C-T-S" stand for adoration, confession, thanksgiving and supplication. All are types of prayer admonished in Scripture, but I think this order is important. We will

"I count all things to be loss in view of the surpassing value of knowing Christ Jesus my Lord, for whom I have suffered the loss of all things, and count them but rubbish so that I may gain Christ."

—The apostle Paul Philippians 3:8

speak more of each of these areas of prayer in the weeks to come. Each will become a theme of one of the weeks of this study. We will grow in our appreciation of the role each part plays in our pursuit of God. For now, I offer them as a guideline for talking with God.

ACTS PRAYING

"A"–ADORATION—Take some time to praise God for who He is, identifying some of His attributes you find particularly meaningful. Express these in a written letter to Him in the space below. Personally, I have found that writing these thoughts out in my journal is so helpful to my worship, for my conscience will not allow me to write words I know that I do not really mean.

Praise God for your
sweetness
mercy
patience
freshness
ability.

"C"–CONFESSION—Remember, don't go looking for something to confess; instead ask God to search your heart and to bring to mind anything that needs to be dealt with especially in this area of walking worthy in your service and seeking of Him.

Confession is not just admitting wrong but seeing it the way God sees it.

> **"You will seek the LORD your God, and you will find Him if you search for Him with all your heart and all your soul."**
>
> **—Moses**
> **Deuteronomy 4:29**

"T"–THANKSGIVING—Thank God for the many blessings of your life and take a moment to ask God what you need to be thankful for.

for answered prayer
for His faithfulness
that I can always depend on Him
for entrusting Kingdom work.

"S"–SUPPLICATION—Pray for God's working in your life in showing you His will and helping you to do it. Bring to Him any requests and needs that are on your heart.

> *Make obvious where my work is, according to Your will.*

Scriptural Prayer to Pray for Yourself and Others

> *For this reason I too, having heard of the faith in the Lord Jesus which exists among you and your love for all the saints, do not cease giving thanks for you, while making mention of you in my prayers; that the God of our Lord Jesus Christ, the Father of glory, may give to <u>you a spirit of wisdom and of revelation in the knowledge of Him.</u> I pray that the eyes of your heart may be enlightened, so that you will know what is the hope of His calling, what are the riches of the glory of His inheritance in the saints, and what is <u>the surpassing greatness of His power toward us who believe.</u> (Ephesians 1:15–19a)*

Main Point to Remember from Day Two:

Growing in a deeper knowing of God is to be our life-long pursuit, but we decide how <u>far we go</u> on that journey.

> *May it always be my desire to go further.*

> **"Let the heart of those who seek the LORD be glad. Seek the LORD and His strength; Seek His face continually."**
>
> **—Asaph**
> **I Chronicles 16:10b–11**

Pursuit **DAY 3**

PURSUING A SIMPLE, PURE DEVOTION

How are we to pursue the Lord? It seems that for many Christians <u>the pursuit of God has become a complicated and intimidating process.</u> But that is the nature of religion, not of true spirituality. God gave Moses the Ten Commandments, but the religious leaders of Israel took those ten instructions and turned them into 642 laws and religious rules. They became self-proclaimed experts on what it took to please God. But when Jesus came, He did not affirm their complicated spirituality. In fact, He went the opposite direction. Instead of complicating rules He simplified them. He reduced the Ten Commandments into one essential commandment—

> *"You shall love the Lord your God with all your heart, and with all your soul, and with all your mind." This is the great and foremost commandment. The second is like it, "You shall love your neighbor as yourself." On these two commandments depend the whole Law and the Prophets. (Matthew 22:37–40)*

Christ basically reduced the law to one word—love. He called us not to a complicated religious ritual, but to simple, pure devotion. The apostle Paul writes, *"But I am afraid, lest as the serpent deceived Eve by his craftiness, that your minds should be led astray from the simplicity and purity of devotion to Christ"* (2 Corinthians 11:3).

This verse's glimpse into Paul's anxious thoughts speaks volumes about spiritual life. His fear is no more unfounded today than it was two millennia ago. First, it tells us we have an adversary, though we'd rather not think about that. Of course, our pursuit of God is not without opposition. There is one who opposes both the Lord and us. His goal is to lead us astray from God. We certainly don't want to think about that. Another disconcerting revelation it offers is that our adversary (Satan) has been successfully doing his job since the beginning of time—starting with his encounter with Adam and Eve in the Garden of Eden. We'd rather not think about that either, but these are things we need to think about if we don't want him to succeed.

This verse has profoundly impacted my walk with God. As I look over and over again at it's startling message, it has caused me to ask myself some probing questions I'm not very comfortable thinking about, let alone actually asking. For instance, this verse's impact has forced me to come face-to-face with my own flawed spirituality and to honestly ask, **"Is my walk with God what He wants it to be?"** Such a question is unsettling, as I'd rather comfortably assume that my walk is in line with what God desires whether such an assumption is accurate or not. If you're like me, you probably don't like to think about such things either, but the Spirit of God isn't going to let us alone.

There is however, a bright side to this verse. With incredible clarity and conciseness, it reveals what our spiritual goal ought to be: simple, pure devotion to Christ. We are called to pursue God Himself, not just morality, service, or knowledge—in other words, such a pursuit is simple, but not easy. God wants us to be pure of heart and wholly devoted. Satan desires to draw us away from this simple, pure devotion. All that is in the devil's world system supports him in this aim. Added to that danger is the distraction of our own fallen nature, which is so easily drawn away. Satan would like nothing better than to tempt us into rebellion, luring us to turn away from our devotion to pursue sin instead. But if rebellion does not work, he is just as satisfied if he can entice us to a pursuit of religiosity. He is contented to have us **busy working for God** if that keeps us from **walking with God**—anything but simple, pure devotion to Christ. Satan delights in religious game playing if it helps us to avoid true worship from devoted hearts. Our call is to seek the Lord—nothing more, nothing less, nothing else. Will we?

FOR ME TO FOLLOW GOD
Write down the main aspect that spoke to you out of today's lesson.

*Remember to pursue God
meditate on that.
what does that look like?
pursuing God.*

"The LORD is with you when you are with Him. And if you seek Him, He will let you find Him."

*—Azariah
2 Chronicles 15:2*

*pure of heart
wholly devoted.*

> " 'You shall love the Lord your God with all your heart, and with all your soul, and with all your mind.' This is the great and foremost commandment."
>
> —Jesus
> Matthew 22:37–38

ACTS PRAYING

"A"–ADORATION—This passage tells us that the secret to a dynamic walk with God is "simple, pure devotion to Christ." Take some time to focus your heart on the One we are to adore. Express His worthiness in your letter to Him.

You are worth more than anything else that I have, do or know.
Without you my life would lack hope and be pointless.

"C"—CONFESSION—Don't go looking for something to confess; just ask God to bring to mind anything that needs to be dealt with. However, be sensitive to any conviction the Spirit is kindling in your heart in this area of pursuit. If you have been led astray from simple, pure devotion, God's arms are open to welcome you back.

Hurried devotional time - find a quiet early unhurried space give what I start with not what is left over.

"T"—THANKSGIVING—Thank God for the many ways He draws you back to simple, pure devotion and for the many benefits of your walk with Him.

- the sweetness of others
- the responsibilty you have trusted me with
- the desire to teach
- the desire to serve.

"S"—SUPPLICATION—Pray for God's help in staying on track in your relationship with Him and for insight into the ways Satan succeeds in leading you astray. Pray for at least one other person God puts on your heart in this area. Ask Him to bring to your mind someone who needs your prayers.

Satan tries to make me feel ashamed but God's truth is liberating not offensive.

Cliff + mom - for salvation.

Scriptural Prayer to Pray for Yourself and Others

One thing I have asked from the Lord, that I shall seek: That I may dwell in the house of the Lord all the days of my life, to behold the beauty of the Lord and to meditate in His temple. For in the day of trouble He will conceal me in His tabernacle; in the secret place of His tent He will hide me; He will lift me up on a rock. Hear, O Lord, when I cry with my voice, and be gracious to me and answer me. When You said, "Seek My face," my heart said to You, "Your face, O Lord, I shall seek." (Psalm 27:4–5, 7–8)

Main Point to Remember from Day Three:

The devil will do anything he can to keep us from simple, pure devotion to the Lord.

LEARNING WHAT PLEASES THE LORD

Pursuit **DAY 4**

Centuries before Christ, the prophet Micah was used by the Lord to clarify the nature of true spirituality. He posed the very question we have been asking this week. Micah 6:6 asks, *"With what shall I come to the Lord?"* It is a surprising question for a number of reasons. It was surprising because of who was asking it. The inquiry did not originate from the Gentiles or pagans, but with the Jews—the very ones who were supposed to be the experts in the worship of Jehovah. It was also surprising because they were doing the actions of worship while asking the question. Surely, they must have recognized a measure of emptiness in the rituals they were performing. In the verses that followed they asked, *"Shall I come to Him with burnt offerings, with yearling calves?"* In other words, they wanted to know, "Is the **expected** enough?" Next they queried, *"Does the LORD take delight in thousands of rams, in ten thousand rivers of oil?"* Here, they essentially asked, "Is he pleased with the **extravagant**? Finally they requested, *"Shall I present my firstborn for my rebellious acts, the fruit of my body for the sin of my soul?"* Here, they wanted to know, "Shall I bring the **extreme** to show my devotion to God?" The offering of a firstborn child was what the Canaanites did, sacrificing their own children as a burnt offering to the pagan god, Molech.

> **"[Josiah] did right in the sight of the LORD, and walked in the ways of his father David and did not turn aside to the right or to the left. For in the eighth year of his reign while he was still a youth, he began to seek the God of his father David."**
>
> **2 Chronicles 34:2–3a**

Through Micah, God answered His people:

> *He has told you, O man, what is good; and what does the LORD require of you but to do justice, to love kindness, and to walk humbly with your God? (Micah 6:8)*

You see, we complicate our faith when we focus on actions and rituals, but God simplifies it by drawing our eyes back to the proper heart attitude. What does God require? He requires us to do justice, love kindness (mercy) and to walk humbly with Him. This summary covers all our important relationships. To *"do justice"* speaks of what we should expect in relation to ourselves. We should want to do the right thing in our hearts. To *"love kindness"* or mercy speaks of how we relate to others. We should delight in showing mercy to others (which is how God treats us), not in demanding justice. Finally, to *"walk humbly"* clearly speaks of how we relate to God. When we recognize His greatness, it ought to create an appropriate humility in our hearts. It is within our hearts—the core of our being—that true spirituality exists, or else it doesn't exist at all.

The apostle Paul expressed this same principle in the New Testament, where he writes, *"You were formerly darkness. But now you are light in the Lord: Walk as children of light (for the fruit of the light consists in all goodness and righteousness and truth), trying to learn what is pleasing to the Lord"* (Ephesians 5:8–10).

Often, trying to live the Christian life is made difficult as we begin to focus on everything that needs to be off-limits. We begin creating our list of "Thou shalt nots" and struggle with trying to live up to them. The result is a spiritual life that is increasingly complicated. This isn't surprising; the Pharisees did the exact same thing. At one point (Matthew 23:23), Jesus told them they were tithing *"mint and dill and cummin"* (imagine worrying about giving a tenth of the spices you grew!), and yet they neglected the weightier provisions of the law: *"justice and mercy and faithfulness."* He called them blind guides who *"strain out a gnat and swallow a camel"* (23:24). In other words, they were putting the priority on the wrong things. Here in Ephesians, Paul simplifies the Christian life considerably.

In these verses, Paul tells us we are *"children of light"* in the Lord. The Christian life, therefore, is simply a matter of living consistent with that. He divides the "fruit of light" into three categories: That which is **good**, that which is **right**, and that which is **true**. These are the things we must major on in the Christian life. How do we do that? Simply put, we are to always try to learn *"what is pleasing to the Lord."* As we face a choice, "What would please the Lord?" As we are given an opportunity, we should always ask, "What would please the Lord?" In fact, in every situation and circumstance we could ask ourselves that same question for it sums up what Lordship is all about.

FOR ME TO FOLLOW GOD

Write down the main thing you need to do differently today as a result of this lesson.

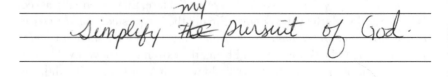

Simplify ~~the~~ my pursuit of God.

_____

_____

_____

_____

_____

_____

ACTS PRAYING

"A"–ADORATION—Take some time to praise God for who He is, identifying some of His attributes you find particularly meaningful and express these in your letter to Him. A good passage to meditate on today if you have time is Psalm 139.

> _powerful_
> _clear thinking_
> _consistent_
> _loving_
> _long suffering_
> _generous_
> _listens_
> _answers_

"C"–CONFESSION—Remember, don't go looking for something to confess; instead ask God to search your heart and to bring to mind anything that needs to be dealt with, especially in this area of pleasing Him instead of pleasing yourself. Ask God what would please Him in your present circumstances.

> _focus on Christ not on pleasing_
> _others or gaining the approval_
> _of others!_

"T"—THANKSGIVING—Thank God for the many benefits of your walk with Him and for being His child (not just His servant). Take a moment to ask God what you need to be thankful for.

> "He has told you, O man, what is good; and what does the LORD require of you but to do justice, to love kindness, and to walk humbly with your God?"
>
> —The prophet Micah
> Micah 6:8

My Husband
my children
work that is enjoyable.

"S"–SUPPLICATION—Pray for God's working in your life in helping you learn what pleases Him, what is good and right and true (2 Chronicles 31:20–21). Ask Him to help you be an imitator of Him. Pray God would give those in your family a heart to want to know what pleases Him.

> "As for me, I would seek God, and I would place my cause before God; Who does great and unsearchable things, wonders without number."
>
> **—Job**
> **Job 5:8**

Scriptural Prayer to Pray for Yourself and Others

> *Keep back Your servant from presumptuous sins; let them not rule over me; then I will be blameless, and I shall be acquitted of great transgression. Let the words of my mouth and the meditation of my heart be acceptable in Your sight, O Lord, my rock and my Redeemer. (Psalm 19:13–14)*

Main Point to Remember from Day Four:
Part of what it means to pursue the Lord is trying to learn what pleases Him.

Pursuit **DAY 5**

PICTURES OF PURSUING GOD

As we look at what the Bible records of the people who have followed God, we find the principle of personal devotions modeled over and over. We see in the lives of the saints as well as the Savior, the choice to carve out time to spend with God. One of the real benefits of Scripture is that it doesn't just tell us what to do, or even why to do it, but it also shows us how. If we want to know what it means to walk with God, we need to start with Jesus. God took on human frailties so He could show us the life

He created for us. I can't fully understand how God could spend time with Himself, but in Jesus' humanity, we see modeled a perfect pursuit of God reflected in the priority of time with Him. In Mark 1:35 we read, *"In the early morning, while it was still dark, Jesus got up, left the house, and went away to a secluded place, and was praying there."* This verse is somewhat brief, yet it speaks volumes about the priority Jesus placed on spending time alone with God the Father. In the busyness of His public ministry, Christ got up while it was still dark. He sacrificed time; He took initiative. We know from the context (see Mark 1:32) that the night before had been a hectic one. The entire city had gathered where He was staying, bringing their sick and demon-possessed. He probably ministered late into the night, yet the next morning He got up early to spend time with God. I have heard attributed to Martin Luther a quote concerning prayer in the midst of a hectic life: "Busy, busy, busy; work, work, work. I have so much to do today, I must spend the first three hours in prayer." The busier our lives get, the more we need time with God to keep things in proper perspective. Jesus went out into the wilderness, to a secluded place. He intentionally left the house where He was staying. We find in the verses that follow that everyone was looking for Him, and His disciples eventually found Him. Imagine how short His time with God would have been if He had stayed at the house. He wisely found a place free from distraction and interruption, where He could talk with God. There are a lot of practical principles for us today in His example.

While the Gospel of Mark records this instance as a specific event, it is clear that it was not an isolated event. When Jesus went with His disciples to Gethsemane to pray, Luke uses the phrase, *"as was His custom"* to describe it (Luke 22:39). Morning was not the exclusive time that Jesus set aside to spend with the Father, either. Mark 14:23 says that after Jesus sent the crowds to whom He had ministered away, *"He went up on the mountain by Himself to pray, and when it was evening, He was there alone."* For Jesus, time with God was a priority, but He was flexible enough to adjust to the changing schedule of a busy life.

Maybe you are thinking, "Sure, Jesus had a quiet time, but after all, He is God." Consider then the decidedly human example of David. He was called *"a man after [God's] heart"* (Acts 13:22). Over the course of his life, he developed a deeply intimate and personal relationship with God as reflected in the many psalms he wrote. In Psalm 5:1–3 we read, *"Give ear to my words, O Lord, consider my groaning. Heed the sound of my cry for help, my King and my God, for to You I pray. In the morning, O Lord, You will hear my voice; in the morning I will order my prayer to You and eagerly watch."* We see that he talked with God in the morning, but also that he listened—his habit was to *"eagerly watch."* In Psalm 63:1, David exclaims, *"O God, You are my God; I shall seek You earnestly."* Psalm 92:1–2 reads, *"It is good to give thanks to the Lord and to sing praises to Your name, O Most High; to declare Your lovingkindness in the morning and Your faithfulness by night."* Apparently David's time with God could be morning or evening or both. These would seem to be the most logical times to meet with God, either at the beginning of our day or at the end of it. Each of these verses we've looked at give us a glimpse of what made David's faith what it was.

Another model we find in Scripture of meeting with God is the life of Moses. In Exodus 33:7–11, we learn that Moses used to pitch a tent a good distance outside the camp as a place for people to meet with God. It is interesting that this principle of a quiet place, free from distraction was observed all the way back to Moses' day. God would speak to Moses in that tent of

"Busy, busy, busy; work, work, work. I have so much to do today I must spend the first three hours in prayer."

—attributed to Martin Luther

meeting. The pillar of cloud, a visible manifestation of God's presence, would hover over that tent, and when the people saw that cloud, they would worship (verse 10). When we practice the principle of personal devotions, we have something Moses and Israel did not have. We have the written word of God for Him to speak to us. Yet the principle of meeting with God remains the same.

FOR ME TO FOLLOW GOD

As you consider today's truth, is there some specific area where you know you need to grow?

- consistency in devotions
- prioritizing
- loving others

"Seek the Lord while He may be found; Call upon Him while He is near."

—The prophet Isaiah

Isaiah 55:6

ACTS PRAYING

"A"–ADORATION—Take some time to praise God for who He is, identifying some of His attributes you find particularly meaningful and expressing those attributes in a heartfelt letter to Him. A good passage to meditate on today is Psalm 63.

availability
longs to be with me
cares about me
loves me

"C"–CONFESSION—Don't go looking for something to confess; in an act of faith, invite God to bring to mind anything that needs to be dealt with, especially in light of the need to pursue the Lord.

"T"–THANKSGIVING—Thank God for the many blessings of your life, taking a moment to ask God to name some things for which you need to be thankful.

parents
grandparents
family
opportunities to grow.

"S"—SUPPLICATION—Pray for God's working in your life in helping you to make time with Him in prayer and in the Word the priority it ought to be. Pray for others in your life that they, too, would resolve to improve in this area.

> "The only way to keep a broken vessel full is to keep the faucet running."
>
> —D. L. Moody

Scriptural Prayer to Pray for Yourself and Others

With all my heart I have sought You; do not let me wander from Your commandments. Your word I have treasured in my heart, that I may not sin against You. Blessed are You, O LORD; teach me Your statutes. With my lips I have told of all the ordinances of Your mouth. I have rejoiced in the way of Your testimonies, as much as in all riches. I will meditate on Your precepts and regard Your ways. I shall delight in Your statutes; I shall not forget Your word. (Psalm 119:10–16)

Main Point to Remember from Day Five:
If we keep our hearts prepared to receive God's Word, each seed that is sown will further our growth.

THE CALL OF A DISCIPLE

D o you feel "called" today? Do you realize that you have been invited to follow the Lord as a disciple? For most of us, it is easy to place a great distance between ourselves and the original followers of Jesus. Perhaps such thinking is understandable in light of the amount of time that has passed since the days Jesus walked and talked with His disciples. Yet with that barrier of time, we often sterilize our reading of Scripture as if life were completely different then and people were different too. We subtly convince ourselves that these men who followed Jesus were the exception rather than the rule. We fool ourselves into thinking that we could never be what they were. Yet we are very much like them. Human nature has not changed, nor has human need. The call to follow echoes just as loudly today, and the possibility is just as real. God desires that we be disciples, and He invites us to follow Him.

When Jesus called the twelve to follow Him, He called them to a specific purpose. It wasn't just a general invitation to come and hang out with Him, but a specific challenge to follow Him in His mission.

> *And He appointed twelve, that they might be with Him, and that He might send them out to preach. . . . (Mark 3:14)*

In this explanation of Jesus' call to His original twelve disciples we can learn much about what it means for us to be a disciple or follower of Jesus today. With simple reflection we see that you can divide Jesus' call into two integral components: **a)** that the disciples might be with Him, and **b)** that He might send them out to preach. They were called to know Him and to make Him known. Jesus appointed these men to be His first disciples, but He invites us to follow Him as well. Both of these aspects of His call are essential to a healthy walk with God. First and foremost, we must develop our relationship with God. That is why we have begun this study with an emphasis on pursuit. But it doesn't stop there. Knowing Him means learning from Him and following His example, which automatically leads us to ministry. Jesus said, *"Follow Me, and I will make you fishers of men."* Following Christ always leads to ministry. If not, we are not fully following Him.

Jesus spent three years with the twelve disciples and with others who chose to follow Him. From the beginning, the invitation was *"Come and see"* (John 1:39). For the first year or so, He expected them to do little else besides build a relationship with Him. He invited them into His life and let them observe. Toward the end of that time He began giving them small, manageable tasks. This was followed by a second invitation: *"follow Me"* (Mark 1:17). This is when Jesus formalized His relationship with them. He took responsibility for their growth and training. He continued, *"And I will make you fishers of men."* During this next phase, as they continued spending time with Him, He sent them out for ministry. He desires to do the same with us. It is not that He needs our help. He could reach the world just fine without us. But He invites us to join Him in His work. That is the very thing we were created to do, and we will never be fulfilled simply receiving from Him. We are made to give out to others.

In the holy lands, there are two major bodies of water: the Sea of Galilee and the Dead Sea. The two are connected by the Jordan River, and yet they are

"I gave my attention to the Lord God to seek Him by prayer and supplications, with fasting, sackcloth and ashes."

—The prophet Daniel
Daniel 9:3

vastly different. One, the Sea of Galilee, is known for supporting a thriving fishing industry. The other, the Dead Sea, cannot even support life. What makes the difference between the two? Both are fed by the same water, so why so different a result? The key is in what they do with what they receive. The Sea of Galilee takes in its water from the north and transfers it to the south. The Dead Sea takes that same water from the north and does nothing with it, so it stagnates and dies. Christians are a lot like that. There are two ways to choke off our spiritual life. One is to choke off the supply end, our relationship with Christ, and we eventually end up with an empty well. The other is for us to not give out what God pours in, and the result is a well that is full, but stagnant and lifeless. For us to experience the abundant life Christ promised, those rivers of living water He pours in us must flow out of us in ministry. That is what it means to be one of His disciples.

FOR ME TO FOLLOW GOD

Write down the main idea that personally spoke to you from today's lesson.

_____

_____

_____

_____

_____

_____

_____

_____

_____

ACTS PRAYING

"A"–ADORATION—Take some time to praise God for who He is, identifying some of His attributes you find particularly meaningful and express these attributes in a letter to Him. A good thing to meditate on today is the concept of knowing God (that we might *"be with Him"*).

_____

_____

_____

_____

_____

_____

_____

_____

"C"–CONFESSION—Remember, don't go looking for something to confess; instead ask God to search your heart and to bring to mind anything that needs to be dealt with especially in the areas of knowing God and ministry.

> **"It is time to seek the LORD until He comes to rain righteousness on you."**
>
> **—The prophet Hosea**
> **Hosea 10:2**

means believing God. not with out sin

_____
_____
_____
_____
_____
_____
_____
_____

"T"–THANKSGIVING—Thank God for the many blessings of your life; take a moment to ask God to identify some things for which you need to be thankful.

_____
_____
_____
_____
_____
_____
_____
_____
_____

"S"–SUPPLICATION—Pray for God's working in your life in living out through ministry what He establishes in you through your relationship with Him. Bring to Him any requests and needs that are on your heart. Pray for others that are important to you.

_____
_____
_____
_____
_____
_____
_____
_____

"Seek the Lord that you may live."

—The prophet Amos

Amos 5:6

Scriptural Prayer to Pray for Yourself and Others

> *For this reason I bow my knees before the Father, from whom every family in heaven and on earth derives its name, that He would grant you, according*

to the riches of His glory, to be strengthened with power through His Spirit in the inner man, so that Christ may dwell in your hearts through faith; and that you, being rooted and grounded in love, may be able to comprehend with all the saints what is the breadth and length and height and depth, and to know the love of Christ which surpasses knowledge, that you may be filled up to all the fullness of God. (Ephesians 3:14–19)

Main Point to Remember from Day Six:
God calls us first and foremost to be with Him, and from that He sends us out to minister to others.

THE STEPS OF OUR PURSUIT

Scripture often compares our pursuit of God with the running of a race. In 1 Corinthians 9:24–27 Paul writes,

Do you not know that those who run in a race all run, but only one receives the prize? Run in such a way that you may win. Everyone who competes in the games exercises self-control in all things. They then do it to receive a per-ishable wreath, but we an imperishable. Therefore I run in such a way, as not without aim; I box in such a way, as not beating the air; but I discipline my body and make it my slave, so that, after I have preached to others, I myself will not be disqualified.

We want to pursue God, but we also desire to be sure we are doing it the right way. We want to "run in such a way that we may win."

The writer of the book of Hebrews paints a graphic and motivating portrait of what it means to pursue the Lord. He writes, *"Therefore, since we have so great a cloud of witnesses surrounding us, let us also lay aside every encumbrance, and the sin which so easily entangles us, and let us run with endurance the race that is set before us, fixing our eyes on Jesus, the author and perfecter of faith. . ."* (Hebrews 12:1–2a).

Here we find four keys of what it means to "run the race" of the Christian life. Verse 1 gives us the dramatic imagery of the Christian life as a race. The stands are filled with those who have already run the race, who are cheering us on (including the Old Testament saints who are listed in Hebrews chapter 11). We are those at the starting line waiting for our own race to start. This exhortation serves as a practical application to the biographies of chapter 11. Here we find four key words all beginning with the letter "E," each one emphasizing an essential to walking by faith or "running the race" as verse 1 puts it.

The first call Hebrews gives us is to *"also lay aside every ENCUMBRANCE."* The Olympic runner of ancient Greece would strip off all his clothes in preparation for his race to insure that he had freedom of movement. In the same way, we must strip down our lives of things that would slow us down in our pursuit of being pleasing to God. The word "encumbrance" means a mass or weight, and in this verse it doesn't necessarily refer to sin, but to things that would hinder us in our race. Can you imagine an Olympic sprinter trying to run the 100-meter dash wearing a business suit and wing–tip shoes while carrying a brief case? Such an athlete would have lit-

> **"Seek the LORD, all you humble of the earth who have carried out His ordinances"**
>
> **—The prophet Zephaniah Zephaniah 2:3**

tle hope of out-distancing those who were more properly attired. For success in our pursuit of God, we must lay aside everything that slows us down.

The next call we find in Hebrews 12 is to lay aside *"the sin which so easily ENTANGLES us."* All sin entangles and trips us up in the race, but this verse refers not to sins in general but to "the" sin. In light of the context, falling on the heels of chapter 11's treatise on faith, this probably refers to the sin of unbelief, or not trusting God and taking Him at His word in a given situation. Unbelief is sure to trip us, bringing our progress in the race to a halt. If we reflect honestly on sin, we quickly realize that every sin is rooted in unbelief. At its core, our choice to rebel against the Lord's will and way is made because we doubt Him and His goodness. If we are to pursue the Lord, we must lay aside the sin of unbelief that so easily entangles us. *"Without faith, it is impossible to please Him"* (Hebrews 11:6).

The third call here is to *"run with ENDURANCE"* the race set before us. The Christian life isn't a sprint, but a marathon. It isn't won by a sudden burst of expended energy but by the slow, steady progress of continuing step by step and staying on the course. It is the call to keep coming back to God no matter how many times we stumble on the path or stray from it. The Christian life is often referred to as a "walk." That means that it consists of a lot of steps in the same direction. Every day we must choose to keep taking steps toward Him—we must pursue Him.

The final call we find in Hebrews 12 is to be *"fixing our EYES on Jesus, the author and perfecter of faith."* Jesus is the origin, the example, the champion and the finisher of our faith. Focusing our eyes on Him reveals encumbrances that need to be laid aside. It alerts us to the entangling sin of unbelief, and it also helps us to run with endurance, to not grow weary and lose heart. We must always keep Jesus in view, or we won't look at life with His perspective. Losing sight of Jesus will cause us to be ineffective runners in the race. All week we have considered one central theme—the principle of pursuit. Time with God is essential. If we really want to know Him, we will pursue Him day by day.

"Seek first His kingdom and His righteousness, and all these things will be added to you."

—Jesus
Matthew 6:33

FOR ME TO FOLLOW GOD

Write down the main idea that spoke to you personally from today's lesson.

_____

_____

_____

_____

_____

_____

_____

_____

_____

_____

ACTS PRAYING

"A"–ADORATION—Take some time to praise God for who He is by identifying some of His attributes you find particularly meaningful and expressing these attributes in a letter to Him. You may want to make use of a praise tape or some familiar choruses.

_____
_____
_____
_____
_____
_____
_____

"C"–CONFESSION—Remember, don't go looking for something to confess; instead ask God to search your heart and to bring to mind anything that needs to dealt with especially in this area of running the race of the Christian life.

_____
_____
_____
_____
_____
_____
_____
_____
_____
_____

"T"–THANKSGIVING—Thank God for the many blessings of your life; take a moment to ask God to identify some things for which you need to express heartfelt gratitude.

_____
_____
_____
_____
_____
_____
_____
_____
_____
_____

> *"One like a Son of Man . . . was given dominion, glory and a kingdom, that all the peoples, nations, and men of every language might serve Him."*
>
> *Daniel 7:13, 14*

"S"–SUPPLICATION—Pray for God's working in your life in showing you His will and helping you to do it. Bring to Him any requests and needs that are on your heart. Ask Him to bring to mind one person you can pray for.

_____

_____

_____

_____

_____

_____

_____

_____

_____

"He is a rewarder of those who seek Him."

—The unknown author of Hebrews
Hebrews 11:6

Scriptural Prayer to Pray for Yourself and Others

Give ear to my words, O Lord, consider my groaning. Heed the sound of my cry for help, my King and my God, For to You I pray. In the morning, O Lord, You will hear my voice; in the morning I will order my prayer to You and eagerly watch. Let all who take refuge in You be glad, let them ever sing for joy; and may You shelter them, that those who love Your name may exult in You. For it is You who blesses the righteous man, O Lord, You surround him with favor as with a shield. (Psalm 5:1–3, 11–12)

Main Point to Remember from Day Seven:

The pursuit of the Christian life requires laying aside encumbrances and entanglements, running with endurance, and keeping my eyes on the Lord.

Main Things to Remember from the Principle of Pursuit:

❑ Each day God reveals something new of His love for us, and we don't want to miss it.

❑ Growing in a deeper knowing of God is to be our life-long pursuit, but we decide how far we go on that journey.

❑ The devil will do anything he can to keep us from simple, pure devotion to the Lord.

❑ Part of what it means to pursue the Lord is trying to learn what pleases Him.

❑ If we keep our hearts prepared to receive God's Word, each seed that is sown will further our growth.

❑ God calls us first and foremost to be with Him, and from that He sends us out to minister to others.

❑ The pursuit of the Christian life requires laying aside encumbrances and entanglements, running with endurance, and keeping our eyes on the Lord.

The Main Question to Ask Myself Is:

Am I pursuing God?

Week Two

The Principle of Adoration

The last verse of the last psalm begins with the statement, *"Let everything that has breath praise the Lord."* Perhaps for extra emphasis, the verse concludes with the statement, *"Praise the Lord!"* (Psalm 150:6). You would think that praise of God would not have to be commanded or even suggested. It seems that the worship and adoration of our Creator would be the normal and natural activity of all creation. Yet even though humans have been placed at the height of creation—bearing the image of God Himself, endowed by the Creator with the greatest capacity for reason and reflection—we still must be reminded to praise the Lord. Why is this so? Why do we not embrace worship of God as the only natural and logical response to all He has done? Tragically, mankind has for the most part achieved an overdeveloped sense of self-worth and has missed the obvious point that the creature owes everything he or she has and is to the One who created him or her. The apostle Paul states in the book of Romans that God's *"invisible attributes, His eternal power and divine nature, have been clearly seen, being understood through what has been made"* (Romans 1:20). In other words, everywhere we look we see the greatness of God reflected. Every corner of creation and every creature He has made give evidence of our Lord's greatness, goodness, and power. The question is, "What will we do with this knowledge?" Seeing clearly God's attributes, power, and nature ought to move us quickly to praise. Our hearts should overflow with adoration of Adonai, yet often we do not acknowledge this as we should.

> **"Let everything that has breath praise the Lord. Praise the Lord!"**
>
> **—Psalm 150:6**

In Romans, Paul tells us clearly what happens to those who suppress the truth of God that is revealed to them. Paul writes,

> They are without excuse. For even though they knew God, they did not honor Him as God or give thanks, but they became futile in their speculations, and their foolish heart was darkened. Professing to be wise, they became fools, and exchanged the glory of the incorruptible God for an image in the form of corruptible man and of birds and four-footed animals and crawling creatures (Romans 1:20–23).

To know God in truth requires us to honor Him for who He is and to give thanks for all He has done, the only reasonable response of thinking people. If we refuse to do so, we become *"futile"* in our thinking—we lose sight of our created purpose, and everything in life becomes meaningless. Paul tells us that those who reject what God reveals of Himself will find that their *"foolish"* hearts have become darkened with sin. Self-absorbed in their so-called wisdom, they become fools.

As humans, we were created for worship. In fact, every living thing was created to offer worship to God. As we read in Psalm 150, *"everything that has breath"* is to praise the Lord. This truth especially applies to men and women alike. In Revelation 4:11 we read, *"Thou hast created all things, and for Thy pleasure they are and were created"* (KJV). God created human beings for His pleasure. All of humanity have an innate need to worship. In fact, it is guaranteed that everyone will worship something or someone. Those who choose not to worship God will exchange the glory of God (the Creator) for something unworthy of worship that has been created. They will worship themselves (whom God created), their talents (which God gave), gold (which God created), or something else undeserving of glory.

At this point you may be thinking, "I'm glad I'm not like those unbelievers." But even believers can fail to give God the glory due His name. In fact, I would go so far as to say that we **always** fall short of what God deserves. However great our view of Him is, He is infinitely greater still. Whatever feeble praise we offer, He is deserving of far more. In the entire universe, He alone is worthy. I find that this is the easiest aspect of our faith to overlook. In the words of the great theologian A. W. Tozer, worship is "the missing crown jewel" in our faith. We pursue God; we confess our sins to Him; we give Him thanks for what He does for us; we make our requests concerning what we want Him to do for us; but true adoration is often the one thing we omit. In our self-centered pursuits, we think mostly of ourselves instead of the One who made us. That needs to change. This week, we will focus on the principle of adoration and doing all we can to make room for it in our hearts.

Adoration DAY 8

GRASPING THE GREATNESS OF GOD

In First John 3:1, we find this powerful statement: *"See how great a love the Father has bestowed on us, that we would be called children of God; and such we are."* Think about what this is saying. God loves us so much that He calls us his children. Truly, we are God's beloved. What an encouragement this is! The God who created us and is our Master has every right to relate to us as slaves. Instead, He wants to relate to us as family. This was probably a difficult concept for the ancient Jews to understand. I'm sure their eyes popped wide open when Jesus told them to call God "Abba." That was the Hebrew equivalent of "Dada," the first word a baby might learn to speak. What a blessed encouragement it is to be part of God's family! But this same passage also holds some words of great challenge.

> *Beloved, now we are children of God, and it has not appeared as yet what we will be. We know that when He appears, we will be like Him, because we will see Him just as He is. (1 John 3:2)*

John tells us that when Jesus appears, *"we will be like Him, because we will see Him just as He is."* This verse offers tremendous hope, and certainly it is cause for rejoicing; however, consider the flip side of that coin. If seeing Him as He is will cause us to become like Him, then the other side of that truth is that we obviously do not yet truly see Him as He is. Whatever our view of God is, it is inadequate and incomplete. Job tells us, *"Behold, these are the fringes of His ways, and how faint a word we hear of Him! But His mighty thunder, who can understand?"* (Job 26:14). What beauty and awesomeness we see in these *"fringes"* we have glimpsed of Him! What an incredible thought that the majesty we worship is so much less than the reality we will one day fully comprehend! But so far, our view of Him is hardly accurate. We cannot begin to comprehend His greatness, might, and power. We have only a scant knowledge of His love and beauty. In the words of J. B. Phillips, "Our God is too small" (that is to say, our view of Him is too small). God is far bigger, far greater than our limited minds can imagine. The good news, though, is that the more our view of God grows and the more our understanding of Him comes into focus, the more we will become like Him. Seeing God does a transforming work in our lives.

Worship is the acknowledgment of who God is. Though we should readily admit that God is infinitely greater than any description or praise of Him we can muster, our worship acknowledges His glory. It acknowledges that we are only vessels to be used by Him at His discretion. Worship is not vain flattery—it is not **exaggerating** who God is, but rather, **reflecting more accurately** who He is—the almighty, most holy Lord who is worthy of all praise. Because our minds are imperfect, we are prone to forget that God is infinitely greater than human comprehension; therefore, we must continually remind ourselves of God's greatness through our worship. One of the reasons we need to practice the principle of adoration is so that we can be daily reminded of God's majesty and glory. If we lose sight of God's greatness, our faith will weaken. It is no wonder we lose heart when we lose vision.

In the preface to his classic book, *The Knowledge of the Holy,* A. W. Tozer says, "The church has exchanged her once lofty concept of God and has substituted for it one so low, so ignoble, as to be utterly unworthy of thinking, worshiping men." We need to regain our lofty view of God.

FOR ME TO FOLLOW GOD

Write down the main idea that spoke to you personally from today's lesson.

_____

_____

_____

_____

_____

"Behold, these are the fringes of His ways; and how faint a word we hear of Him! But His mighty thunder, who can understand?"

—Job
Job 26:14

> **"Worship the Lord with reverence and rejoice with trembling."**
>
> **—Psalm 2:11**

ACTS PRAYING

"A"–ADORATION—Take some time to praise God for who He is, identifying some of His attributes that you find particularly meaningful and expressing these characteristics in a letter to Him in the space provided below. You may want to make use of a praise tape or some familiar choruses. If you have time, read Job 36 and reflect on all that it reveals of God. Remember, we begin with adoration, focusing on who God is. This not only reminds us of His greatness, but also should move our hearts toward an appropriate humility and reverence as we converse with Him.

_____

_____

_____

_____

_____

_____

_____

"C"–CONFESSION—Remember, don't go looking for something to confess; instead, ask God to search your heart and bring to your mind anything that needs to be dealt with, especially in this area of your adoration of Him. If you feel that your heart has lacked a true worship of Him, acknowledge this.

_____

_____

_____

_____

_____

_____

_____

"T"–THANKSGIVING—Thank God for the many blessings of your life, including His grace and work in and through you, and take a moment to ask Him to identify some things for which you need to offer heartfelt thanks.

_____

_____

_____

_____

_____

_____

_____

"S"–SUPPLICATION—Pray for God to work in your life by showing you His will and helping you to do it. Bring to Him any requests and needs that are on your heart. Pray for others to become worshipers of God.

_____

_____

_____

_____

_____

_____

_____

Praying Scripture

> *Now to Him who is able to do far more abundantly beyond all that we ask or think, according to the power that works within us, to Him be the glory in the church and in Christ Jesus to all generations forever and ever. Amen. (Ephesians 3:20–21)*

Main Point to Remember from Day Eight:
No matter how great our view of God is, He is greater still—we have not yet seen Him as He truly is.

"To You, O God of my fathers, I give thanks and praise."

—Daniel

Daniel 2:23

Giving God the Glory He Deserves

Adoration DAY 9

In Romans 13:7, the apostle Paul instructs us, *"Render to all what is due them: tax to whom tax is due; custom to whom custom; fear to whom fear; honor to whom honor."* In other words, make sure you are not deficient in giving to others what you ought to give. We don't always do as we should, and sometimes we don't give others what they deserve. Nowhere is this deficiency more inappropriate than when we withhold from God what He deserves. In Malachi, the Lord rebukes His people, saying, *" 'A son honors his father, and a servant his master. Then if I am a father, where is My honor? And if I am a master, where is My respect?' says the Lord of hosts"* (Malachi 1:6). It is a serious question that we must ask ourselves: "Have I given God the honor and glory He deserves?" If not, this debt must be paid and this problem remedied.

> *Tell of His glory among the nations, His wonderful deeds among all the peoples. For great is the Lord, and greatly to be praised; He also is to be feared above all gods. For all the gods of the peoples are idols, but the Lord made the heavens. Splendor and majesty are before Him, strength and joy are in His place. Ascribe to the Lord, O families of the peoples, ascribe to the Lord glory and strength. Ascribe to the Lord the glory due His name; bring an offering, and come before Him; worship the Lord in holy array." (1 Chronicles 16:24–29)*

How do I give God the honor and glory He deserves? One way is to tell others how great He is—to *"tell of His glory among the nations, His wonderful deeds among all the peoples."* But it is not enough to tell others how great our

> *"Arise, bless the Lord your God forever and ever! O may Your glorious name be blessed And exalted above all blessing and praise! You alone are the Lord."*
>
> *—The Levites Nehemiah 9:5–6*

God is; we must tell **Him.** The Lord is great and *"greatly to be praised."* Offering praise to God is something that should be woven into every conversation we have with Him. Every time we meet with Him, we should adore Him. We have a responsibility to *"ascribe to the Lord the glory due His name."* We owe Him that.

We are not the only beings who give God glory, but we may be the only ones who withhold it from Him. In Psalm 19:1, we are told, *"The heavens are telling of the glory of God."* The vast expanse of the universe constantly speaks a silent sermon of God's glory. In Revelation 4, we learn that four living creatures always stand before the throne of God—Isaiah calls them *"seraphim"* (see Isaiah 6:12). Day and night, these creatures unceasingly give glory and honor and thanks to Him who sits on the throne, saying, *"Holy, holy, holy, is the Lord God, the Almighty, who was and who is and who is to come"* (Revelation 4:8). Verse 4 of this same chapter informs us that twenty-four elders sit on thrones encompassing the throne of the Lord. They appear to be from the realm of mankind—the leaders of the twelve tribes of Israel and the twelve apostles, because these leaders have gates and foundation stones named after them in the New Jerusalem (see Revelation 21). These twenty-four elders fall down before God and worship Him. The day will come when they cast their golden crowns at His feet saying, *"Worthy are You, our Lord and our God, to receive glory and honor and power; for You created all things, and because of Your will they existed, and were created"* (Revelation 4:11). In Revelation 5, we learn that when Christ breaks the seven seals on the book of judgment, myriads upon myriads and thousands upon thousands of angels will be *"saying with a loud voice, 'Worthy is the Lamb that was slain to receive power and riches and wisdom and might and honor and glory and blessing' "* (Revelation 5:12). Do you get an idea of what this verse implies? They aren't speaking these praises in normal tones; they are shouting it—saying it with a *"loud voice"*! Immediately after this event takes place, every created thing that is in heaven and on the earth and under the earth and on the sea, and all things in them, will be heard saying, *"To Him who sits on the throne, and to the Lamb, be blessing and honor and glory and dominion forever and ever"* (Revelation 5:13). We need not wait until this climactic moment to offer our praise to the One who is worthy of all praise. As the carol implores, "O come let us adore Him"—*now!*

FOR ME TO FOLLOW GOD

Write down the main idea that spoke to you personally from today's lesson.

_____

_____

_____

_____

_____

_____

_____

_____

_____

_____

_____

ACTS PRAYING

"A"–ADORATION—Take some time to praise God for who He is, identifying some aspects of His worth that you find particularly meaningful. Then express these aspects in a letter to Him. You may want to sing to Him the familiar Christmas carol, "O Come All Ye Faithful." (Yes, you can sing this song any time of the year!) Remember, He is worthy of glory and honor, and we are called to *"ascribe to the Lord the glory due His name."* Make your adoration an offering you bring to Him.

_____

_____

_____

_____

_____

_____

_____

_____

_____

"C"–CONFESSION—Be sensitive to any shortcomings that you may have in giving God the glory He is due. Confess to Him any other area of sin that is afflicting you, but don't forget to also acknowledge that God is the author of forgiveness.

_____

_____

_____

_____

_____

_____

_____

"Where is He who has been born King of the Jews? For we saw His star in the east and have come to worship Him."

—The Magi Matthew 2:2

"T"–THANKSGIVING—Thank God for the many blessings of your life, and take a moment to ask Him to name some areas for which you should offer special thanks.

_____

_____

_____

_____

_____

_____

_____

_____

> "I will bless the Lord at all times; His praise shall continually be in my mouth. My soul will make its boast in the Lord; the humble will hear it and rejoice. O magnify the Lord with me, and let us exalt His name together."
>
> —David
> Psalm 34:1–3

"S"–SUPPLICATION—Pray for God to work in your life in this area of adoration. Bring to Him any requests and needs that are on your heart. Pray for others to become worshipers of God.

_____

_____

_____

_____

_____

_____

_____

_____

_____

_____

Praying Scripture

Holy, holy, holy, is the Lord God, the Almighty, who was, and who is, and who is to come. . . . Worthy are You, our Lord and our God, to receive glory and honor and power; for You created all things, and because of Your will they existed, and were created. . . . Worthy is the Lamb that was slain to receive power and riches and wisdom and might and honor and glory and blessing. . . . To Him who sits on the throne, and to the Lamb, be blessing and honor and glory and dominion forever and ever (Revelation 4:8, 11; 5:12–13).

Main Point to Remember from Day Nine

Though our comprehension of God is extremely limited, we can be assured that God is worthy of glory and honor. We have a responsibility to ascribe to Him the glory due His name.

Adoration **DAY 10**

SINGING TO THE LORD

Do you ever sing to the Lord? I am not asking if you sing in church, because that isn't always optional. But when you sing in church, do you sing to the Lord? What about when you are alone with the Lord—does singing ever enter into the equation? The clear message of Scripture is that it should. The word "singing" in its related forms appears nearly 250 times in the Bible. Yet most Christians I speak with never sing unless they have to. Where does song fit into our worship and adoration of God?

It has always been interesting to me that one of the evidences of being a Spirit-filled Christian is singing. Ephesians 5:18 commands us to *"be filled with the Spirit."* In other words, we are called to yield every area of our lives to the control of the Spirit of God. This passage goes on in its next breath to exclaim that those who are Spirit-filled will be *"speaking to one another in psalms and hymns and spiritual songs, singing and making melody with your heart to the Lord"* (Ephesians 5:19). I would have to question, "Is it possible to be Spirit-filled and not sing?" Although we can and do sing without worshiping, do we ever truly worship without a song in our hearts and on our lips?

The psalmist writes, *"Sing to the Lord a new song; sing to the Lord, all the earth. Sing to the Lord, bless His name; proclaim good tidings of His salvation from day to day. Tell of His glory among the nations, His wonderful deeds among all the peoples. For great is the Lord, and greatly to be praised; He is to be feared above all gods"* (Psalm 96:1–4). Notice who is to sing—*"all the earth."* Notice when we are to sing—*"from day to day"* (not just on Sunday). Notice where—*"among the nations . . . among all the peoples."* Notice why—*"for great is the Lord, and greatly to be praised."* He is truly worthy of our vocal praise, and truly, He alone is worthy. We cannot conveniently dismiss this call to sing praise to the Lord. If we believe His Word, then we must bow to it in obedience or else tear those verses that command us to sing right out of our Bibles. Who would be so bold? God tells us to sing. As Jesus says in Luke 6:46, *"Why do you call Me, 'Lord, Lord' and do not do what I say?"* Singing is not optional in the Christian life.

Singing alone offers no guarantee of worship. We can honor Him with our lips and our hearts may still be far from Him. But singing has an uncanny way of giving expression to a surrendered heart. Some things cannot be said—only sung at the top of our lungs. The words to the song, "A Mighty Fortress Is Our God" cannot be whispered. The song "How Great Thou Art" requires the full measure of our voices to be endowed with any meaning at all. By no means am I suggesting that only the old hymns should be sung. I love them, and there is nothing wrong with them, but Psalm 96 calls us to sing *"a new song."* I believe each generation creates new ways to express their praise of God. Some of the best praise I have heard is the ancient words of the Psalms put to contemporary melodies. The Psalms were the Jewish hymnbook. But notice that God recorded for posterity the lyrics, not the tunes. This tells me two things about singing to the Lord. First, the lyrics are the most important part. A song is not effective if it cannot be understood. It must speak truth as much as a sermon or a Scripture reading. Second, there is no one style of music that is more inspired than others. Each generation and each culture is free to find its own musical expression. We can learn to appreciate the musical styles of others, but we must recognize that the Bible puts all of the emphasis on what the songs have to say, not on how it is said. Don't judge others because their musical taste is different from yours.

Purpose in your heart to make singing a part of your encounters with the Lord. I have called this book *How to Develop a Quiet Time,* and for generations the saints have used the term "quiet time" to refer to meeting with God for personal devotions. But I must tell you that, on many occasions, my time spent with the Lord has been anything but quiet. From time to time, I raise my voice to Him, and I invite you to do the same.

FOR ME TO FOLLOW GOD

Write down the main idea that spoke to you personally from today's lesson.

_____

_____

_____

_____

_____

_____

_____

_____

> **"Sing to the Lord, praise the Lord! For He has delivered the soul of the needy one from the hand of evildoers."**
>
> **—Jeremiah Jeremiah 20:13**

"Praise the Lord in song, for He has done excellent things."

—Isaiah
Isaiah 12:5

ACTS PRAYING

"A"–ADORATION—In your time of adoration today, apply (put into action) what you saw in the Word. Sing to the Lord and bless His name. You may want to make use of a favorite CD and sing along with songs that you enjoy and find meaningful. Make sure, though, that you sing them to the Lord. You may find it helpful to keep a hymnal or chorus book handy when you spend time with the Lord.

_____

_____

_____

_____

_____

_____

_____

_____

"C"–CONFESSION—Be sensitive to anything you need to confess related to your thinking and practice of singing. Maybe you are convicted of not singing, or perhaps of not singing to the Lord." Confess to Him any other area of sin in your life and thank God for forgiving you.

_____

_____

_____

_____

_____

_____

_____

_____

T–THANKSGIVING—Thank God for the many blessings of your life, and for who He is. Ask God to show you some obscure things for which you should be eternally grateful.

_____

_____

_____

_____

_____

_____

_____

_____

"S"–SUPPLICATION—Pray for God's continued working in your life in this area of adoration. Ask Him to help you accept the worship styles of others. Bring to Him any requests and needs that are on your heart. Pray for others as God brings them to your mind.

_____

_____

_____

_____

_____

_____

_____

_____

> "About midnight Paul and Silas were praying and singing hymns of praise to God."
>
> —Paul and Silas in the Philippian jail Acts 16:25

Praying Scripture

Even though the following passage was not written as a prayer, its content makes for a great conversation with the Lord. I have personalized the wording of the verses so that the verses lead us into speaking directly to the Lord instead of about Him.

> *I come and sing for joy to You, Lord; I shout joyfully to the rock of my salvation. I come before Your presence with thanksgiving; I shout joyfully to You with psalms. For You are a great God, and a great King above all gods. I come to worship and bow down; I kneel before You, my Lord and Maker. For You are my God, and I am one of the people of Your pasture and the sheep of Your hand." (adapted from Psalm 95:1–3, 6–7)*

Main Point to Remember from Day Ten:

We are called to worship God with song, and when we are Spirit-filled, we do it from our hearts.

HALLOWED BE THY NAME

Adoration **DAY 11**

Perhaps the single most recognized prayer of all time is the prayer our Lord Jesus taught to His disciples in Matthew 6. Many churches pray this prayer every time they gather. And yet, with anything so familiar, there is always the danger of ritual's replacing reason and habit's getting in the way of "hallowing." Familiarity tends to breed contempt. When was the last time you used the word "hallowed" in a conversation, let alone thought about what it truly means? Yet Jesus taught us to pray, *"Our Father who is in heaven, hallowed be Your name"* (Matthew 6:9). What does it mean to "hallow" the name of God? The Greek word used for "hallowed" is *hagiazo*, which means "to sanctify," (to regard and set apart as holy). Certainly we cannot do anything at all to add to the holiness of God, but we can set His name apart as holy and for sacred use. We do this when we speak His name only with reverence and never vainly or flippantly. You see, to hallow the name of God is an attitude in our hearts that is a product of adoration.

Our Father who art in heaven how would you know my name.

> "To the Lord, I will sing, I will sing praise to the Lord, the God of Israel."
>
> —Deborah and Barak
>
> Judges 5:3

Woven into this concept of hallowing the name of God is the idea the Scriptures put forward, of the fear of God. The great A. W. Tozer wrote that the fear of God "may grade anywhere from its basic element—the terror of the guilty soul before a holy God—to the fascinated rapture of the worshipping saint" (Tozer, *Whatever Happened to Worship.* Christian Publications, p.30). Both of these extremes are practical expressions of faith without which it is impossible to please God. Yet Tozer went on to say that this powerful sense of godly fear is a quality missing in the churches of today. Why? I believe it is in part because we have lost the art of adoration. We do not remind ourselves of who God really is. We do not take the time to gaze in appreciation on His greatness. Apart from an adoring reverence for Him (which must be cultivated on the basis of truth and faith in that truth), our Christianity is reduced to mere moralism and our prayers to selfish renderings of a grocery list of what we want done for us. The Lord's Prayer begins with adoration of God and reverence for Him.

Consider the words: *"Our Father . . . hallowed be Your name."* These words speak of a reverence for God Himself. They acknowledge Him as our Father. This tells of Him as our Source—we find our origin in Him. But it is also a message of intimacy and relationship. We acknowledge Him as our Father who is in heaven. Even in this simple statement, we remind ourselves that His place is higher than ours. Adoration begins by speaking truth about God. People may praise each other with excess and hyperbole, but there can be none of this when speaking of God. Whatever praise we offer cannot exceed His greatness but is ever doomed to fall short. True adoration of Him does not merely serve as blessing to Him; it also reminds us of the One to whom we come. Adoration must always shape our supplication. If not, then we fall into a false view of God and cease to hallow His name. God is not a candy machine where we put our contribution in, punch all the right buttons and get from Him what we desire. He is not a cosmic bellhop, with nothing better to do than to serve our wants. He is not a computer search engine ever waiting to answer our inquiries.

In Ecclesiastes, the wise King Solomon warns us,

> Guard your steps as you go to the house of God and draw near to listen rather than to offer the sacrifice of fools; for they do not know they are doing evil. Do not be hasty in word or impulsive in thought to bring up a matter in the presence of God. For God is in heaven and you are on the earth; therefore let your words be few. (Ecclesiastes 5:1–2)

When we approach God with adoration first, it shapes everything else we say (or don't say). It causes us to listen to God's greatness before we speak. It reminds us of who (and where) He is. It helps us to have a reverence for God's priorities and not simply our own. Remember, the Lord's Prayer goes on to implore, *"Your kingdom come. Your will be done, on earth as it is in heaven."* How do we pray? Should we pray about His kingdom or ours? Should we pray for His will or ours? One of the ways we can adore Him is to value Him and to value what He values. Reflect on the Lord's Prayer; not only does it begin with adoration but, as if for added emphasis, it ends with adoration as well: *"For Yours is the kingdom and the power and the glory forever. Amen."*

FOR ME TO FOLLOW GOD

Write down the main idea that spoke to you personally from today's lesson.

_____

_____

_____

_____

_____

_____

_____

_____

_____

ACTS PRAYING

"A"–ADORATION—Continue to include singing and verbal adoration in your time with God. Don't just recite or sing the words; think about what they mean. Give God your undivided attention as you adore Him.

_____

_____

_____

_____

_____

_____

_____

_____

_____

_____

"C"–CONFESSION—Invite God to reveal to your heart anything that stands between you and Him. Confess to Him anything that is convicting you, thanking Him for the forgiveness that is ours in Christ.

_____

_____

_____

_____

_____

_____

_____

_____

_____

_____

_____

"You shall fear only the Lord your God; and you shall worship Him and swear by His name."

**—Moses
Deuteronomy 6:13**

"T"–THANKSGIVING—Thinking always precedes thankfulness. Reflect on all that God has given and done, and thank Him for the many blessings of your life. Ask God to show you blessings for which you need to thank Him.

_____

_____

_____

_____

_____

_____

_____

_____

"S"–SUPPLICATION—Pray for the VIPs in your life—those who are important to you. Ask God to impress on your heart someone who needs to be prayed for today.

_____

_____

_____

_____

_____

_____

_____

_____

_____

_____

> ### "Praise the name of the Lord your God, who has dealt wondrously with you."
>
> ### —Joel
> ### Joel 2:26

Praying Scripture

> _Our Father who is in heaven, hallowed be Your name. Your kingdom come. Your will be done, on earth as it is in heaven. Give us this day our daily bread. And forgive us our debts, as we also have forgiven our debtors. And do not lead us into temptation, but deliver us from evil. For Yours is the kingdom and the power and the glory forever. Amen. (Matthew 6:9–13)_

Main Point to Remember from Day Eleven:

When we talk to the Lord, we must hallow His name and maintain an attitude of adoration.

Adoration | **DAY 12**

THE SIN OF WITHHELD GLORY

On the Sunday before the crucifixion, Jesus made His triumphal entry into Jerusalem—riding on the back of a donkey. Have you ever thought about that event from the perspective of that small donkey? Crowds gathered to see him walk in. People placed their garments on the ground as a carpet for him to walk on. They cheered and waved palm branches as they shouted, *"Hosanna! Blessed is he who comes in the name of the Lord"* (Mark 11:9; John 12:13). This adolescent animal had probably never experienced anything close to such interest in all of its early life. It would have been a pretty foolish donkey, though, to think that the attention was directed at it. The recognition and adoration were aimed at the One who rode on its back. Humankind faces that same kind of circumstance all of the time, yet often fails to hold it in proper perspective. Everything we do, everything we accomplish, every accolade and acclaim directed our way exists because of the One who created us and endowed us with whatever gifts and opportunities we enjoy. Yet often we take the glory for things instead of giving glory to God, who ultimately deserves it.

Our God is a jealous God (see Exodus 20:5). He will not share His glory or worship with another. King Herod learned this the hard way. We learn in Acts 12 that Herod had James put to death and intended to do the same with Peter, but Peter escaped. Some time later, as Herod gave an oration, the people described him as having *"the voice of a god and not of a man"* (Acts 12:22). Instead of correcting them, he accepted for himself the glory that belongs only to God and was judged accordingly. God's judgment of Herod was swift and severe, but the important thing to note is that it was not because of the evil Herod had done to God's people. In Acts 12:23, Luke explains why Herod died an untimely death: *". . . because he did not give God the glory."*

In Daniel 4, we find a similar example of God's dealings with one who wrongly accepted God's glory for himself. Through the prophet Daniel, God warned King Nebuchadnezzar of his pride and withholding of the glory God deserves. Yet the king was unrepentant. A year later, as he gazed from the roof of his royal palace at the glories of his kingdom, Nebuchadnezzar exclaimed, *"Is this not Babylon the great, which I myself have built . . . by the might of my power and for the glory of my majesty?"* (Daniel 4:30). Notice the attitude of the king's heart that these words reveal. We see self-will (*"Is this not Babylon the great, which I myself have built"*), self-effort (*"by the might of my power"*), and self-glory (*"and for the glory of my majesty"*). While these words were still on Nebuchadnezzar's lips, judgment fell. The king lost his mind and, for seven years, wandered as a beast, eating grass like the cattle. Fortunately, the story doesn't end there. Nebuchadnezzar repented. In fact, this chapter of the book of Daniel concludes with King Nebuchadnezzar's own words of testimony: *"At the end of that period I, Nebuchadnezzar, raised my eyes toward heaven, and my reason returned to me"* (Daniel 4:34a). Notice that, though he could not speak, he could still give God glory in his heart by simply raising his vision. Once he did, his mind was restored and he then gave verbal glory to God: *"I blessed the Most High and praised and honored Him who lives forever; for His dominion is an everlasting dominion, and His kingdom endures from generation to generation"* (Daniel 4:34b). When the king repented of the sin of withheld glory, God restored his mind and his majesty and his mission and even added *"surpassing greatness"* to him. What did King Nebuchadnezzar learn from all of this? I'll let him tell you—*"Now I, Nebuchadnezzar, praise, exalt and honor the King of heaven, for all His works are true and His ways just, and He is able to humble those who walk in pride"* (Daniel 4:37). It is a sin to withhold from God the glory He is due.

> *"And when I heard and saw, I fell down to worship at the feet of the angel who showed me these things. But he said to me, 'Do not do that. I am a fellow servant of yours and of your brethren the prophets and of those who heed the words of this book. Worship God.' "*
>
> —John
> Revelation 22:8–9

FOR ME TO FOLLOW GOD

Write down the main idea that spoke to you personally from today's lesson.

_____
_____
_____
_____
_____
_____
_____
_____

"I . . . praise, exalt and honor the King of heaven, for all His works are true and His ways just."

—Nebuchadnezzar Daniel 4:37

ACTS PRAYING

"A"–ADORATION—Continue to make the practice of singing and verbal adoration a habit in your time with God. You may feel more comfortable praying silently, but this is not the same. Some things should be said or sung out loud. You will find that doing so brings you into the Lord's presence in a meaningful way.

_____
_____
_____
_____
_____
_____
_____
_____

"C"–CONFESSION—Ask God to make you sensitive to anything you need to confess following today's study. Confess your sins and thank God for the forgiveness He provides.

_____
_____
_____
_____
_____
_____
_____
_____
_____

"T"–THANKSGIVING—Thank God for the many blessings of your life, and take a moment to ask God what you need to be thankful for. Give Him thanks for His greatness.

_____
_____
_____
_____
_____
_____
_____

"S"–SUPPLICATION—Pray for God's working in your life in guarding you from pride and helping you to see His supremacy. Bring to Him any requests and needs that are on your heart, and pray for others, especially leaders.

_____
_____
_____
_____
_____
_____
_____
_____
_____
_____

Praying Scripture

Why not personalize King Nebuchadnezzar's words and use them as a prayer of adoration to God?

I bless the Most High and praise and honor Him who lives forever; for His dominion is an everlasting dominion, and His kingdom endures from generation to generation. I praise, exalt, and honor the King of heaven, for all His works are true and His ways just, and He is able to humble those who walk in pride. (Based on Daniel 4:34b, 37)

Main Point to Remember from Day Twelve:

It is a sin that God will judge, to withhold from Him the glory He is due.

> _"All the sons of Israel . . . bowed down on the pavement with their faces to the ground, and they worshiped and gave praise to the Lord, saying, 'Truly He is good, truly His lovingkindness is everlasting.'"_
>
> **—2 Chronicles 7:3**

ADORE HIM AS THE ESSENCE OF YOUR LIFE

Adoration **DAY 13**

What gives your life meaning? What is your purpose? What is the "why" in your life? Sadly, many people today can't answer these questions. Their lives have no meaning; they merely exist from

> *"Abraham said to his young men, 'I and the lad will go over there; and we will worship."*
>
> **—Genesis 22:5**

day to day. So they invest great energy in trying to dull the edge of the pain in their lives by balancing the pain with as much pleasure as they can find. They live for the next relationship, the next experience, the next vacation, or the next high. Others have found a purpose for their lives, but it is a wrong one. Some try to find identity in possessions—accumulating great wealth and amassing many things. They climb the ladder of success all the way to the top, only to discover that the ladder is leaning against the wrong wall. Some try to find meaning in their accomplishments. They labor long and hard to achieve power and position, only to learn that the euphoria from attaining power is fleeting and unsatisfying. We were made for worship, and if we do not worship that which is worthy, we will worship something unworthy. The real question is, "What gives my life meaning?"

For the apostle Paul, answering that question was easy. In Philippians 1:21, he relates, *"For to me, to live is Christ and to die is gain."* What a powerful statement Paul makes here! To really appreciate what he is communicating, it is helpful to know a little bit about the Greek language. In New Testament Greek, there are two words for "life." One word, *bios* (from which our English word "biology" is derived), describes mere existence—to be alive. In 2 Timothy 2:4, it is used to refer to the *"affairs of everyday life."* The other word, *zoē,* means "the essence of life" or "the fullness of life." The earliest Greek manuscripts use *zoē* in John 10:10 when Christ says that He *"came that they might have life."* *Zoē* is the same word that Paul uses in Philippians 1:21. What Paul is saying in Philippians 1:21 is thus: "The essence of my life is Christ . . . He is what makes me tick." The phrase *"for to me"* in this verse is translated from an emphatic personal pronoun in Greek; in other words, this is a very personal remark. To fully appreciate Paul's words, you must see the context in which he expresses them. He was in prison, falsely accused and targeted for death because of his witness for Christ. He didn't know if he was going to live or die, but to him it didn't matter. In fact, one of the reasons that he wrote to the Philippians was so they wouldn't worry about him. Paul's attitude is a little difficult to understand. If I were in prison for no good reason, I'd be grumbling and complaining, wanting people to worry about me. But in verse 12, Paul explains that God used his imprisonment to give him more opportunities to minister. Therefore, he could rejoice in his imprisonment.

For Paul, the essence of his life was Christ, not his circumstances. Because of this, Paul could take his eyes off himself in the midst of some very trying circumstances. He found all of his meaning and fulfillment in his relationship with the Lord. But how did he arrive at this? One key is found in the third chapter of Philippians. Paul had just reviewed his resume and his list of credentials (with some credentials earned before his conversion), and he counted every personal accomplishment as nothing (as loss) compared with knowing Christ. In verses 13 and 14 he says, *"Forgetting what lies behind, . . . I press on toward the goal for the prize of the upward call of God in Christ Jesus."* Christ was his life because Christ was his goal. He no longer had the fulfillment of self as his driving objective.

It truly is a paradox that laying aside the pursuit of fulfillment eventually produces fulfillment. To gain my life, I must lose it. To really live, I must die to self and let Jesus **be** Jesus in me. When I do this, my whole life becomes an expression of adoration. When living is worship, what fills my heart begins to show up on my lips. Adoring God is not a ritual to perform but a product of a life given to Him.

FOR ME TO FOLLOW GOD

Write down the main idea that spoke to you personally from today's lesson.

_____

_____

_____

_____

_____

_____

_____

_____

_____

ACTS PRAYING

"A"–ADORATION—Take some time to focus on how worthy God is of our devotion. Praise Him not only in song and in words, but also where it is most important, in your life.

_____

_____

_____

_____

_____

_____

_____

_____

"C"–CONFESSION—Look into your heart, and ask God to show you any areas where you are finding your meaning and satisfaction outside of Him. Repent where necessary.

_____

_____

_____

_____

_____

_____

_____

_____

"Therefore I urge you, brethren, by the mercies of God, to present your bodies a living and holy sacrifice, acceptable to God, which is your spiritual service of worship."

—Paul
Romans 12:1

"T"–THANKSGIVING—Thank God for the truth that you can have His joy regardless of your circumstances, because He is the true essence of your life.

_____
_____
_____
_____
_____
_____
_____
_____

"S"—SUPPLICATION—Pray for God to work in your life so that you consistently look to Him for your meaning, purpose, and joy. Bring to Him any requests and needs that are on your heart.

_____
_____
_____
_____
_____
_____
_____
_____
_____

Praying Scripture

Now to our God and Father be the glory forever and ever. Amen. (Philippians 4:20)

Main Point to Remember from Day Thirteen
Adoring God is not a ritual to perform but a product of a life given to Him.

"Then Israel [Jacob] bowed in worship."

—Genesis 47:31

Adoration **DAY 14**

SEEING OURSELVES IN THE LIGHT OF GOD'S GLORY

"*In the year of King Uzziah's death, I saw the Lord*" (Isaiah 6:1). With these fateful words, the prophet Isaiah begins his explanation of the most pivotal event of his entire life. He would never be the same after this divine encounter of revelation. Isaiah grew up in an influential, upper class family and was a close friend and counselor to King Uzziah. In fact, many scholars believe that Amoz, Isaiah's father was Uzziah's uncle, which would make them cousins. It is shortly after Uzziah's death that God reveals Himself to Isaiah in a supernatural way. Listen to Isaiah's account and try to "put yourself in his shoes":

> *In the year of King Uzziah's death I saw the Lord sitting on a throne, lofty and exalted, with the train of His robe filling the temple. Seraphim stood above Him, each having six wings: with two he covered his face, and with two he covered his feet, and with two he flew. And one called out to another and said, "Holy, Holy, Holy, is the Lord of hosts, the whole earth is full of His glory." And the foundations of the thresholds trembled at the voice of him who called out, while the temple was filling with smoke. Then I said, "Woe is me, for I am ruined! Because I am a man of unclean lips, and I live among a people of unclean lips; for my eyes have seen the King, the Lord of hosts."* (Isaiah 6:1–5)

Why is adoration so important? Because it is seeing God rightly that puts all the rest of life into proper perspective. When I see God, I am then able to see everything else clearly. It seems apparent that there is a relationship between the death of Isaiah's friend, Uzziah, and his encounter with the Lord. Uzziah had been a godly king during the early years of his reign, but he became corrupted as time passed. Uzziah trusted God and saw mighty deliverances, but his successes made him proud, and in his pride he forgot God. Pride led to his undoing, as it had destroyed so many kings before him. There is much in the book of Isaiah to suggest that Uzziah's sin had become an issue in Isaiah's life.

One of the problems with observing the sin of others is that doing so can make it easier for us to view our own sin as insignificant. The first five chapters of Isaiah note that, until the death of Uzziah, the focus of Isaiah's message was on other people. Nine times in those early chapters Isaiah speaks pronouncements of *"Woe"* to this person or that person. But when he sees the Lord, the first words out of his mouth are, *"Woe is me . . . !"* (Isaiah 6:5). Isaiah's response was common among the saints when they gained a clearer view of God (see also Job 42:5–6; Ezekiel 1:28; Daniel 10:8–11; Revelation 4:3). With his eyes on the debauched nation of Israel and its sinful king, his friend Uzziah, the prophet didn't see himself as all that bad. But when he saw the Lord, his perspective completely changed. Isaiah already knew the Lord, but he did not have as reverent a view of God before this encounter as after it. He used terms such as *"lofty"* and *"exalted"* to describe this new view of God he had gained. The message of the seraphim (Isaiah 6:3) reminded him of the holiness and glory of the Lord, leading him to an appropriate adoration of Jehovah.

What practical application for our lives can be found here? It is so effortless to think of ourselves as righteous when we compare ourselves to those around us. Of course we can always find someone less godly to compare ourselves to, but rare is the person who can weigh the faults of another without putting his or her own thumb on the scales. We can easily focus on the most obvious flaws of others and compare them selectively to ourselves, allowing our hearts to deceive us. But when we see the Lord, then we see ourselves as we truly are—sinners in need of a savior. It is interesting to note what Isaiah repents of: *"I am a man of unclean lips"* (Isaiah 6:5). Isaiah was a prophet, and his mouth was the tool of his trade (and perhaps the source of his pride). Yet once he saw the Lord, even his greatest strength was seen as stained. We need to see God as He really is, and adoration helps us to do that. By seeing God in the proper perspective, we are able to see ourselves accordingly. But God reveals our sinfulness for only one purpose—to cleanse it. We cannot clean ourselves up, but once we recognize our need and come to Him, He

> **"This is my God, and I will praise Him; my father's God, and I will extol Him."**
>
> **—Moses Exodus 15:2**

> *"I will exult in the Lord, I will rejoice in the God of my salvation."*
>
> *—Habakkuk*
> *Habakkuk 3:18*

cleanses us. Then, and only then, can He use us. As soon as Isaiah's iniquity was taken away, God invited Him to be used. *"Whom shall I send . . . ?"* the Lord asks in Isaiah 6:8. Isaiah then quickly responds, *"Here am I. Send me!"*

As we close our consideration of the principle of adoration, we can see why it must come before confession. We must see God in adoration to rightly see ourselves. Next week, we will look at the principle of confession.

FOR ME TO FOLLOW GOD

Write down the main idea that spoke to you personally from today's lesson.

_____

_____

_____

_____

_____

_____

_____

_____

ACTS PRAYING

"A"–ADORATION—Take some time to adore the Lord. You may want to sing the hymn "Holy, Holy, Holy" in light of what you learned from Isaiah.

_____

_____

_____

_____

_____

_____

_____

"C"–CONFESSION—Ask God to give you a greater view of Himself and to use that to give you a clearer view of your own sin. Confess to Him anything you sense that He is putting His finger on, and ask Him to cleanse you as He did Isaiah.

_____

_____

_____

_____

_____

_____

_____

"T"–THANKSGIVING—Take time to thank God for the many blessings of your life, and ask Him to identify some specific areas for which you can be thankful. Give Him thanks for His great forgiveness.

_____

_____

_____

_____

_____

_____

_____

"S"–SUPPLICATION—Pray for God to work in your life, guarding you from pride and helping you to focus on Him instead of other people and things. Bring to Him any requests and needs that are on your heart, and pray for others, especially those you know who are unrepentant. Once we recognize our own sinfulness, we are able to pray with greater compassion for others we see in need of God.

_____

_____

_____

_____

_____

_____

_____

Praying Scripture

First, make the prayer of the seraphim your own:

> _Holy, Holy, Holy, is the Lord of hosts, the whole earth is full of His glory._ (Isaiah 6:3)

Next, make Isaiah's prayer your own:

> _Woe is me, for I am ruined! Because I am a man of unclean lips, and I live among a people of unclean lips; for my eyes have seen the King, the Lord of hosts._ (Isaiah 6:5)

_____

_____

_____

_____

_____

_____

_____

_____

"Give glory to the Lord, the God of Israel, and give praise to Him. . . ."

**—Joshua
Joshua 7:19**

"Through Him then, let us continually offer up a sacrifice of praise to God, that is, the fruit of lips that give thanks to His name."

—The unknown writer of Hebrews
Hebrews 13:15

Main Point to Remember from Day Fourteen:
We must see God in adoration to rightly see ourselves.

Main Ideas to Remember about the Principle of Adoration:

❏ No matter how great our view of God is, He is greater still—we have not yet seen Him as He truly is.

❏ God is worthy of glory and honor, and we have a responsibility to ascribe to Him the glory due His name.

❏ We are called to worship God with song, and when we are Spirit-filled we do it from our hearts.

❏ When we talk to the Lord, we must hallow His name and maintain an attitude of adoration.

❏ It is a sin to withhold from God the glory He is due.

❏ Adoring God is not a ritual to perform but a product of a life given to Him.

❏ We must see God in adoration to rightly see ourselves.

The Main Question to Ask Myself Is:
Do I take time to adore the Lord?

Week Three

THE PRINCIPLE OF CONFESSION

One of the foundational principles of a relationship with God is the principle of confession. It is closely related to the principle of conviction—the two go hand in hand. Conviction is the work of God, and confession is our appropriate response to that work. Confession of our faults and failings is an important step because it keeps our fellowship with God healthy and deals with issues that wall us off from God. We do not begin with confession, however, because starting there would quickly lead to introspection. As we considered last week, when we pursue God, we must begin with adoration of Him. When we adore and worship God we become aware of any sin that needs to be confessed, but our focus is on God, not on sin. We see as much of our sin as we need to see when our eyes are on Jesus. As we saw with Isaiah, when our eyes are on others, we may not see our own sin as we should. And when our eyes are on ourselves, we may see too much of sin. We face the danger of becoming hair-splitting legalists who read sin into everything and may end up focusing on the wrong issues altogether. Jesus said of the Pharisees—the legalists of His day—*"You blind guides, who strain out a gnat and swallow a camel"* (Matthew 23:24). In other words, because their focus was on themselves instead of God, they majored on the minor things and minored on what was really important. When our eyes are on God, we will see the sin He is revealing.

> **"Only acknowledge your iniquity, that you have transgressed against the Lord your God."**
>
> **—Jehovah**
> **Jeremiah 3:13**

How do we know if God is convicting us of sin? This is a truly important question to ask. I believe with all my heart that most of the problems we encounter in spiritual growth and dealing with sin are the results of responding to the wrong voices instead of listening to the voice of conviction—the Spirit of God who lives in us. We often listen to the voice of condemnation from the enemy or the voice of concession from the relative and constantly shifting human morality. It is important when dealing with sin that we recognize the difference between the Holy Spirit's conviction and Satan's condemnation. Conviction is always very specific ("This is what you did wrong") and has repentance and restoration in view. Condemnation, on the other hand, is always general ("You are a bad person"), and its goal is to keep you down and miserable. Conviction looks to the future (repentance and restoration). Condemnation looks to the past (guilty emotions, feelings of failure and worthlessness). In Philippians, the apostle Paul explains what our attitude should be: *"Brethren, I do not regard myself as having laid hold of it* [spiritual maturity] *yet; but one thing I do; forgetting what lies behind and reaching forward to what lies ahead, I press on toward the goal for the prize of the upward call of God in Christ Jesus"* (Philippians 3:13–14). We don't have to live in past failures.

As we consider this principle of confession, a problem arises. We know we are to confess our sins, but what are they? I believe most of us operate from a deficient view of sin. We think of it only in terms of morality. One of the issues we will consider this week is areas of sin we need to confess that we may not readily identify as sin. Keep an open heart to what the Lord may reveal.

Confession **DAY 15**

INVITING GOD TO CONVICT US OF SIN

"Search me, O God, and know my heart; try me and know my anxious thoughts; and see if there be any hurtful way in me, and lead me in the everlasting way."

—King David
Psalm 139:23–24

The secret to continued intimacy with God is quickly dealing with offenses against Him—keeping short accounts with Him regarding sin. If there is something that stands between us and Him, He is ready and willing to reveal that. John 16 tells us that one of the ministries of the Holy Spirit is to *"convict the world concerning sin, righteousness and judgment"* (John 16:8). When He does convict us, we must respond with confession. If we do, the sin will be put behind us and no longer affect our fellowship with God. If we do not respond to the convicting of the Spirit, however, our hearts will become hardened, and we will not enjoy intimacy with the Father.

In Psalm 139, we gain a glimpse of one of the reasons why David could be called "a man after God's own heart." He was willing to let God convict him of his sins. In fact, he invited God to do so. He recognized his need to deal with the sins that would naturally creep into his life. James tells us that *"we all stumble in many ways"* (James 3:2). Not even mighty King David was able to avoid sinning, yet he had a heart after God's heart because he was willing to let God deal with his sins. He didn't try to deal with his sin in his own power, nor did he even try to find sin in his heart. Instead, he invited God to shine the searchlight of His Holy Spirit into the dark corners to find any dirt that needed to be removed.

King David serves as a good model of how to keep a clean heart. If we desire to live a life pleasing to God, it is essential that we open our hearts to Him and let Him cleanse them. Remember, though, it is God's job to find the sin, not ours. Often Satan sneaks us into the trap of introspection—looking for sin in everything we do. If he cannot tempt us into sin, then he will try to discourage us by causing us to focus on ourselves, looking for sin in every attitude and action. The result is condemnation, discouragement, and frustration. He robs us of our joy by saddling us with the responsibility of judging our own hearts. Realize however, that this is an impossible task. Jeremiah lamented, *"The heart is more deceitful than all else and is desperately sick; who can understand it?"* (Jeremiah 17:9). In other words, if we try to search our own hearts, we will fail. Either we will find sin where there is none, resulting in enslavement to legalism, or we will justify away our sin, resulting in further license.

Only God can judge our hearts accurately. After telling us of the deceitfulness in our own hearts, the book of Jeremiah goes on to say, *"I, the Lord, search the heart, I test the mind"* (Jeremiah 17:10). That is why Paul said, *"I do not even examine myself . . . but the One who examines me is the Lord"* (1 Corinthians 4:3–4). David showed us how this can happen—by calling on the Lord to search our hearts. If we sincerely desire to please the Lord, we can be confident that as we seek Him, His Holy Spirit who dwells in us will reveal any sin that stands in the way of fellowship with the Father.

FOR ME TO FOLLOW GOD

Write down the main idea that spoke to you personally from today's lesson.

_____

_____

_____

_____

_____

_____

_____

_____

_____

_____

ACTS PRAYING

"A"–ADORATION—Take some time to praise God for who He is by identifying some of His attributes that you find particularly meaningful and expressing these in a letter to Him. A good passage to meditate on today is Psalm 139, especially David's adoration of God that precedes his prayer.

_____

_____

_____

_____

_____

_____

_____

_____

"C"–CONFESSION—Remember, don't go looking for something to confess; instead, ask God to search your heart and bring to your mind anything that needs to be dealt with.

_____

_____

_____

_____

_____

_____

_____

_____

"And He, when He comes, will convict the world concerning sin, and righteousness, and judgment."

—Jesus, speaking of the Holy Spirit John 16:8

"T"–THANKSGIVING—Thank God for the many blessings of your life, taking a moment to ask Him what you need to be thankful for.

_____

_____

_____

_____

_____

_____

_____

"S"–SUPPLICATION—Pray for God to work in your life as you strive to keep short accounts with Him regarding your sin. Bring to Him any requests and needs that are on your heart.

_____

_____

_____

_____

_____

_____

_____

_____

Search me, O God, and know my heart; try me and know my anxious thoughts; and see if there be any hurtful way in me, and lead me in the everlasting way. (Psalm 139:23–24)

Main Point to Remember from Day Fifteen:
It is God's job to convict us of sin, but our job to respond with confession.

CONFESSION AND REPENTANCE

Confession DAY 16

The term "confession" takes me back to a conversation I had with one of my drinking buddies before I met Christ. In honesty, one day, he told me that he was considering leaving his parent's church to join the one his uncle attended. When I asked him why, he replied, "He's Catholic, and they can get drunk, and it is okay." I was skeptical. "Really," I asked, "they don't think getting drunk is wrong?" He explained that his uncle told him that Catholics believe all you have to do is go to confession after committing a sin, and everything is okay. Since he didn't want to give up drinking, he wanted to be a Catholic instead of a Baptist. (I'm sure that a Roman Catholic priest would offer a different perspective on confession than what my confused friend explained.) But what is confession? Can we live in overt rebellion as long as we tell someone about it and wipe the slate clean once in a while? That is not what God says about confession.

In 1 John 1:9, we find these words, *"If we confess our sins, He is faithful and just to forgive us our sins and to cleanse us from all unrighteousness."* The Greek word for "confess" here (*homologeō*) means "to say the same thing" or, in other words, "to agree." We are to confess and say the same thing about our sin that God says. He says it is wrong. We must agree with Him that it is wrong, and this always includes repentance. If we are unwilling to repent of our wrongful actions, then we don't truly agree that hthey are wrong, and we haven't really confessed. God says sin is to be forsaken. When I come to God in confession, I come in agreement. I come saying the same thing about my sin that He says. I need to acknowledge that it should be forsaken. If I come in confession while planning to commit the same sin again, then I misunderstand what true confession is.

In the same passage John says, *"If we say that we have fellowship with Him and yet walk in the darkness, we lie and do not practice the truth; but if we walk in the Light as He Himself is in the Light, we have fellowship with one another, and the blood of Jesus His Son cleanses us from all sin"* (1 John 1:6–7). The key word here is "walk." One who walks in darkness—whose lifestyle is darkness and who doesn't desire light—is not truly in agreement with God. One who walks in the light may occasionally stray into darkness but does not stay there. He or she leaves the darkness behind with confession. When the darkness is left behind in this way, God is *"faithful and just to forgive us our sins and to cleanse us from all unrighteousness."* You see, He doesn't just want to take away the penalty; He wants to take away the sin.

You may wonder, "Why do I need to confess if my sins were forgiven when I became a Christian?" We are forgiven of all sin—past, present, and future, when we meet Christ. This forgiveness ensures a permanent relationship

> **"If we confess our sins, He is faithful and righteous to forgive us our sins and to cleanse us from all unrighteousness."**
>
> **—John**
> **1 John 1:9**

with the Lord that will not change. But it does not guarantee that we will always enjoy the full benefits of that relationship. The sun always shines, but it is possible to be hidden from its light. Unconfessed sin does not change our relationship with God; He is still our Father who loves us. But it does affect our fellowship with Him. Confession is necessary to restore that broken fellowship. When we confess, we draw His forgiveness and cleansing into our daily experience.

When Jesus wanted to wash the disciples' feet, at first Simon Peter refused. *"Never shall You wash my feet!"* he exclaimed. Jesus answered, *"If I do not wash you, you have no part with Me"* (John 13:8). Then Peter went to the opposite extreme, saying, *"Lord, then wash not only my feet, but also my hands and my head"* (verse 9). Jesus' response gives us a good understanding of confession after salvation: *"He who has bathed needs only to wash his feet, but is completely clean"* (John 13:10). In other words, once your whole body has been cleansed, you only need to deal with the dirt of the day. Confession is maintaining our cleanness before God so that our fellowship with Him is not hindered in any way.

Many of us still walk loaded down with the guilt of sins we have committed. We may have agreed that they are wrong, but we have never agreed with God that they are forgiven. As an application of this lesson, take out a separate sheet of paper. On that sheet, write down every sin that God brings to mind. You don't need to become introspective, looking for sin in every action or attitude. Just invite the Lord to search your heart and bring to your mind anything that is unresolved. Whatever the Lord brings to mind write it down. Once you feel that you are finished, write "1 John 1:9" across the page. Then, as a marker in your own mind, burn the sheet of paper as a reminder that God considers those sins gone. Thank Him for His love and forgiveness! You see, if confession is agreement, we must agree that sin is wrong, we must agree that it needs to be forsaken, but we must also agree with God that it is forgiven.

FOR ME TO FOLLOW GOD
Write down the main idea that spoke to you personally from today's lesson.

_____
_____
_____
_____
_____
_____
_____
_____
_____
_____
_____
_____
_____

"I said, 'I will confess my transgressions to the Lord'; and You forgave the guilt of my sin."

**—King David
Psalm 32:5**

ACTS PRAYING

"A"–ADORATION—Take some time to praise God for who He is by identifying some of His attributes that you find particularly meaningful and expressing these in a letter to Him.

_____

_____

_____

_____

_____

_____

_____

"C"–CONFESSION—Remember, as you confess what you are convicted of is wrong, confess or agree that it is wrong (if you can do that honestly). Confess that it needs to be forsaken, but also remember to confess that it is forgiven.

_____

_____

_____

_____

_____

_____

_____

_____

"T"–THANKSGIVING—Thank God for the many blessings of your life. Thank Him for His forgiveness.

_____

_____

_____

_____

_____

_____

_____

_____

_____

_____

_____

_____

_____

_____

_____

_____

_____

_____

_____

"Although our iniquities testify against us, O Lord, act for Your name's sake!"

—Jeremiah Jeremiah 14:7

Praying Scripture

Although our iniquities testify against us, O Lord, act for Your name's sake! . . . We know our wickedness, O Lord, the iniquity of our fathers, for we have sinned against You. Do not despise us, for Your own name's sake; do not disgrace the throne of Your glory; remember and do not annul Your covenant with us. Are there any among the idols of the nations who give rain? Or can the heavens grant showers? Is it not You, O Lord our God? Therefore we hope in You. (Jeremiah 14:7a, 20–22)

Main Point to Remember from Day Sixteen:

Confession means to agree with God and is always accompanied by repentance.

Confession   DAY 17

DRAWING ON GRACE SO WE CAN ADMIT OUR SIN

Each of us stands always and only by the grace of God. Apart from this, we would never be able to please Him. Yet we do not always draw on the vast reservoir of grace available to us. We see some sin in our hearts, but we are too proud to face it; instead, we try to blame someone else for our own sin. Pride keeps us from admitting our faults and causes us to *"come short"* of God's grace. The writer of Hebrews exhorts us, *"See to it that no one comes short of the grace of God; that no root of bitterness springing up causes trouble, and by it many be defiled"* (Hebrews 12:15). If we come short of God's grace, we will not truly confess (agree with God) about what is sin in our lives. Instead, we will look for someone else to blame for our sinful actions. In our hearts we will say, "Yes, I did this, but it was because of what this other person did (or didn't do) to me." We use the blame we credit to someone else to justify our wrong actions, and we are able to reconcile the guilt of our consciences for a time.

Unfortunately, blame does not take away our guilt. It may bring the scales of conscience into balance, but by adding weight to the other side instead of taking the weight of guilt away. The resulting by-product of blame is that we develop a root of bitterness in our hearts toward the person or persons we try to hold responsible for our own sinful actions. If this bitterness remains unchecked, Hebrews tells us that *"trouble"* will result, , and *"many* [not just us] *are defiled by it."* If we are not experiencing God's grace, then we cannot honestly face our own imperfections through confession. Likewise, if we come short of God's grace for ourselves, we cannot give grace to others. Instead, we demand that they be perfect. When they aren't, we become bitter over their shortcomings, all because our pride keeps us from humbling ourselves and admitting that we need God's grace and forgiveness. James tells us *"God is opposed to the proud, but gives grace to the humble"* (James 4:6). To receive God's grace into our experience, we must humble ourselves and admit (confess) our sin. If we do, we experience the blessing mentioned in Hebrews 13:9, which tells us that God's grace strengthens our hearts. Grace enables us to carry the weight of our own imperfections because we know that, although we are imperfect, we are also forgiven. Admitting our imperfections makes it easier to accept the imperfections of others.

Is there a root of bitterness in your heart toward someone? If so, the problem may well be that you are blaming them for something you need to deal with God about. Or it may be that they are wrong and in need of grace from you, but your lack of experiencing God's grace prevents you from giving it to others. Take a look at the parable in Matthew 18:21–35. In it we find a servant pleading for mercy and being forgiven a debt of ten thousand talents. (A single talent represented more than fifteen years wages for a laborer.) Yet this same man turned around and refused to forgive a fellow slave who owed him a hundred denarii (about a hundred days' wages) and had him thrown into prison. This story reveals a good deal of the human tendency in dealing with sin. We want grace for ourselves, but we don't want to give it to others. How dare we who are so needy of grace from God demand justice for one another? See to it that you do not come short of God's grace—either in receiving it for yourself or in giving it to others. To the crowd who wanted to stone the woman caught in adultery, Jesus said, *"He who is without sin among you, let him be the first to throw a stone at her"* (John 8:7). Soon there was no one left to condemn her.

You see, when we reflect honestly on our own sin—when we are reminded of our own need for forgiveness—we become less eager to sit as judge on the sins of others. It is only by drawing on God's grace that we are able to fully embrace all from which we have been forgiven. This in turn makes us more able to give grace to others, for we recognize in them our own sins, which are many. We treat them as we want to be treated by the Lord. The practice of true confession requires humility, but having drawn on grace, we are then enabled to become agents of God's grace to others.

FOR ME TO FOLLOW GOD
Write down the main idea that spoke to you personally from today's lesson.

_____

_____

_____

_____

_____

"So it shall be when he becomes guilty in one of these, that he shall confess that in which he has sinned."

—Instructions from the Law Leviticus 5:5

_____

_____

_____

_____

_____

_____

_____

ACTS PRAYING

"A"–ADORATION—Take a few minutes to acknowledge God's sovereign right to supremacy both in our world and in our hearts. Worship Him as King as you write your prayer to Him.

_____

_____

_____

_____

_____

_____

_____

_____

_____

_____

"Blessed are the pure in heart, for they shall see God."

—Jesus
Matthew 5:8

"C"–CONFESSION—Don't go looking for something to confess; instead, ask God to search your heart and bring to your mind anything that needs to be dealt with. Remember, God gives grace to the humble.

_____

_____

_____

_____

_____

_____

_____

_____

_____

"T"–THANKSGIVING—Thank God for the many benefits of your walk with Him and for His grace and forgiveness. Take a moment to ask God what you need to be thankful for.

_____
_____
_____
_____
_____
_____
_____
_____
_____
_____

"S"–SUPPLICATION—Pray for God to work in your life, helping you to receive His grace and to give it to others. Pray for someone you are bitter toward or who holds bitterness toward you, that he or she will experience God's grace.

_____
_____
_____
_____
_____
_____
_____
_____
_____
_____

> *"Then Jerusalem was going out to him, and all Judea and all the district around the Jordan; and they were being baptized by him in the Jordan River, as they confessed their sins."*
>
> ## Matthew 3:5–6

Praying Scripture

(Below are prayers Ezra prayed in public confession for the nation of Israel.)

> *O my God, I am ashamed and embarrassed to lift up my face to You, my God, for our iniquities have risen above our heads and our guilt has grown even to the heavens. . . . After all that has come upon us for our evil deeds and our great guilt, since You our God have requited us less than our iniquities deserve, and have given us an escaped remnant as this . . . O Lord God of Israel, You are righteous, for we have been left an escaped remnant, as it is this day; behold, we are before You in our guilt, for no one can stand before You because of this. (Ezra 9:6, 13, 15)*

Main Point to Remember from Day Seventeen:

True confession requires humility and gives us practical access to God's grace.

PRESERVING THE UNITY OF THE SPIRIT

S in separates. One of its effects is the fracturing of human relationships. I am called to love God with all my heart, soul, mind, and strength; but I am also called to love my neighbor as myself. Sin gets in the way of that. Sin separates me from others, whereas the Spirit unifies me with others. As we consider the principle of confession, we must accept the possibility that we have committed some relationship sins that we have not yet recognized. They may be sins of omission instead of commission. They may include the neglect of relationships through selfishness, or the fracturing of relationships because of pride and unforgiveness and demanding our own way. It may be that we sin by what we don't do instead of by what we do. Sin happens in our relationships when Christ is not in control of us.

In Ephesians 4:1–3, the apostle Paul writes, *"Therefore I, the prisoner of the Lord, implore you to walk in a manner worthy of the calling with which you have been called, with all humility and gentleness, with patience, showing tolerance for one another in love, being diligent to preserve the unity of the Spirit in the bond of peace."* He reminds us of our responsibility to live consistently with what we profess to believe and highlights what that looks like. With a fleeting look at the call to *"walk in a manner worthy,"* we may think this speaks of service, but these really are relationship verses. To walk worthy requires of us humility and patience. It demands that we *"show tolerance for one another in love."* In particular, we learn that there is a *"unity of the Spirit"* we must preserve. Note that we are not told to **produce** unity, but rather to **preserve** it. At a glance this may seem insignificant, but consider it further, and it becomes a very important exhortation. First, it tells us that unity already exists in the Spirit. If the same Spirit is Lord of two different hearts, there will automatically be unity. Second, we see that this unity must be preserved. In other words, if we aren't careful, it can be spoiled. Third, we are exhorted to apply diligence to see that God's unity remains intact in His body. This is lived out with the qualities mentioned in verse 2: humility, gentleness, patience, and tolerance. But where do I find such attributes?

In Galatians 5:22–23, we learn that these and many other worthwhile qualities are the result of God's Spirit directing our life. Paul writes that *"the fruit of the Spirit is love, joy, peace, patience, kindness, goodness, faithfulness, gentleness, self-control; against such things there is no law."* If I'm walking in the Spirit, dealing with sin as it shows up in my life and yielding myself to God daily, then this fruit will be manifested in ever-increasing dimensions. I will love others. My joy and peace will be a blessing to them. I'll be patient with them. I'll be good and faithful and gentle. Because I exercise self-control, they won't suffer the consequences of an uncontrolled self. On the other hand, the end of the day may reveal a different story. I may have to confess that instead of giving the blessings of the Spirit in my relationships, I have withheld them from my neighbor, my family, and all whose paths I crossed.

The only way for disunity to creep in is for one of us to take over the rule of our heart. Take a moment to reflect and ask yourself, "Who is Lord of my heart? What is the fruit of my life—is it the fruit of the Spirit of God or the fruit of self? Are any of my relationships strained because unity has not been preserved?" You don't need to be introspective, but invite the Lord to bring to your mind any unity that needs to be preserved (or repaired). It may be that your sin toward others has not found expression but exists in an unlov-

> *"I implore you to walk in a manner worthy. . . . being diligent to preserve the unity of the Spirit in the bond of peace."*
>
> **—Paul**
> **Ephesians 4:1, 3**

ing or judgmental attitude. Do you ever struggle with judging other Christians? With evaluating the quality of their obedience? In Romans 14:4, Paul very clearly and concisely addresses this issue: *"Who are you to judge the servant of another? To his own master he stands or falls; and he will stand, for the Lord is able to make him stand."* A Christian has no business judging another Christian for one major reason: the other person is the servant of another. Although we can encourage one another in the body, submit to one another in love, and hold each other accountable, we are not responsible for each other's faithfulness. This seems to be Jesus' point in John 21:22. Peter was worrying about someone else and Jesus responded, *"If I want him to remain until I come, what is that to you? You follow Me!"* In other words, stop worrying about someone else's faithfulness and focus on your own.

One of the reasons God doesn't want us judging each other is because we are unable to do it fairly. In 1 Corinthians 4:5, we are told that when God judges, He will do it fairly because He will look at the motives of the heart. Humans aren't privy to that information, so we cannot possibly judge another with complete fairness. We will either be too lenient or too harsh. Judging others also creates pride. This was the problem of the Pharisee who prayed, *"God, I thank You that I am not like other people"* (Luke 18:11). God does not compare us to other people, but to Christ, and when He does, all are found wanting. We all have sinned, and we all fall short of God's glory. The flesh wants to derive our value from comparing ourselves to others, rather than from evaluating our own likeness to Christ. The good news from Romans 14:4 is that, though each of us stands or falls to his or her own master, our Master, the Lord, is able to make us stand! Alleluia!

FOR ME TO FOLLOW GOD

Write down the main idea that spoke to you personally from today's lesson.

_____

_____

_____

_____

_____

_____

_____

_____

_____

_____

_____

ACTS PRAYING

"A"–ADORATION—Take some time to praise God for who He is by identifying some of His attributes that you find particularly meaningful and expressing these in a letter to Him.

_____

_____

_____

_____

> *"The Pharisee . . . was praying . . . :'God, I thank You that I am not like other people. . . .'"*
>
> ## Luke 18:11
>
> God does not compare us to other people, but to Christ, and when He does, all are found wanting.

_____
_____
_____
_____

"C"–CONFESSION—Don't go looking for something to confess; just ask God to bring to your mind anything that needs to be dealt with. If God brings to your mind something you have done to get in the way of unity, deal with it before the Lord, and with the other person (or persons) involved. If you are struggling with judging others, take it to Jehovah.

_____
_____
_____
_____
_____
_____
_____
_____

"T"–THANKSGIVING—Thank God for the many benefits of your walk with Him and for the joy of unity with other believers. Take a moment to ask God what (and whom) you need to be thankful for.

_____
_____
_____
_____
_____
_____
_____
_____

"For I confess my iniquity; I am full of anxiety because of my sin."

—King David
Psalm 38:18

"S"–SUPPLICATION—Pray for God's help in preserving the unity of your relationships with other believers, and pray for someone with whom you are having difficulty experiencing unity.

_____
_____
_____
_____
_____
_____
_____
_____

But now, O Lord, You are our Father, we are the clay, and You our potter; and all of us are the work of Your hand. Do not be angry beyond measure, O Lord, nor remember iniquity forever. (Isaiah 64:8–9)

Main Point to Remember from Day Eighteen:

We are called to preserve the unity of the Spirit and must confess when we have not done that.

THE CONSEQUENCES OF UNCONFESSED SIN

Confession **DAY 19**

There are wrong ways to deal with sin and a right way. I'd like you to think about that today. It is such an important subject, because you and I regularly deal with sin, but do we deal with it the right way? One of the wrong ways we address sin is trying to hide it. We sweep it under the rug instead of putting it under the blood of Jesus. Although sin was born in the Garden of Eden, the Genesis 3 story has as much to do with how Adam and Eve responded to their failure as with the failure itself. Once they recognized their sin, Adam and Eve showed consciousness of their sinful state when they attempted to hide their nakedness from each other by covering themselves with fig leaves. Next, they attempted to hide from God among the trees of the garden.

It is our natural flesh response to seek to hide when we sin. This tendency alienates us from other believers and from God and gets in the way of putting the sin behind us. Pride never wants to be found out. Humility, on the other hand, is quick to take responsibility for failure. Adam and Eve hid, but sadly, that is not the only mistake they made in dealing with sin. We see in Adam's response to God that with one statement he tried to shift the blame for his sin to both Eve and God. He said, *"The woman* [blaming Eve] *whom You gave to be with me* [blaming God]*, she gave me from the tree, and I ate"* (Genesis 3:12). Eve took the same approach, trying to shift the blame onto Satan by saying, *"The serpent deceived me, and I ate"* (Genesis 3:13). Our human tendency is to blame someone else, instead of taking responsibility for our sins.

Centuries later another biblical character modeled these same mistakes in dealing with his sin. David was king of Israel and a man after God's own heart, but he was also a sinner. In deceptive strategies that rival the Watergate scandal, he made attempt after attempt at a cover-up of his adulterous affair with Bathsheba. He called Uriah, Bathsheba's husband, home from the war, hoping that Uriah would sleep with her and that the pregnancy resulting from the adultery could be attributed to him. When this cover-up didn't work, David got Uriah drunk, but to no avail. The errant king's last ploy was to have Uriah abandoned in the heat of the battle, which resulted in the soldier's death, adding murder to David's list of sins. When he then took Bathsheba as his wife, the nation thought it an act of kindness to a fallen comrade. His sin was hidden; that is, it was hidden from all but God and David. Think about that. God knew what David did. When we hide our sin, we willfully ignore the fact that God always knows. This truth raises the question, "If God already knows, then why do I need to confess?" The answer ought to be obvious. God knows we need to face our own sin—to admit it instead of hiding it.

"How blessed is he whose transgression is forgiven, whose sin is covered!"

—King David Psalm 32:1

Listen to David's testimony of the consequences of not confessing: *"When I kept silent about my sin, my body wasted away through my groaning all day long. For day and night Your hand was heavy upon me; my vitality was drained away as with the fever heat of summer"* (Psalm 32:3–4). Even if we get away with sin, we don't really get away with it. God told Adam and Eve that if they ate the forbidden fruit, in the day that they ate it they would *"surely die."* They didn't instantly die physically, and for a brief while may have thought they had gotten away with something. But soon they realized that the death was in their spirit. David tasted that same death. But he also learned the right way to deal with sin. In Psalm 32, he relates, *"How blessed is he whose transgression is forgiven, whose sin is covered! How blessed is the man to whom the Lord does not impute iniquity, and in whose spirit there is no deceit! . . . I acknowledged my sin to You, and my iniquity I did not hide; I said, 'I will confess my transgressions to the Lord'; and You forgave the guilt of my sin"* (Psalm 32:1–2, 5).

God knows we need to confess our sin. Unless we agree with Him that our actions are wrong, we will never be able to put them behind us. What qualified David as a man after God's own heart is not the absence of sin in his life—no one but Jesus ever accomplished that. David's heart for God was seen in his brokenness and repentance over his sin. He wanted more from God than to escape the consequences. He prayed, *"Create in me a clean heart, O God, and renew a steadfast spirit within me"* (Psalm 51:10). We come to God in confession after our sin, not just to be forgiven, but also that we may be cleansed and restored.

FOR ME TO FOLLOW GOD

Write down the main idea that spoke to you personally from today's lesson.

_____

_____

_____

_____

_____

_____

_____

_____

ACTS PRAYING

"A"–ADORATION—Take some time to praise God for who He is by identifying some of His attributes that you find particularly meaningful and expressing these in a letter to Him. A good passage to meditate on today is Psalm 133.

_____

_____

_____

_____

_____

_____

_____

_____

"How blessed is he whose transgression is forgiven, whose sin is covered!"

—King David Psalm 32:1

"C"–CONFESSION—Remember, don't go looking for something to confess; instead, ask God to search your heart and bring to your mind anything that needs to be dealt with. Be willing to recognize any hiding of sin or blaming of others.

_____

_____

_____

_____

_____

_____

_____

_____

"T"–THANKSGIVING—Thank God for the many blessings of your life, taking a moment to ask Him what you need to be thankful for.

_____

_____

_____

_____

_____

_____

_____

_____

"S"–SUPPLICATION—Pray for God to work in your life by helping you to be honest with Him and to keep short accounts with Him regarding your sin. Bring to Him any requests and needs that are on your heart. Take time to pray for others.

_____

_____

_____

_____

_____

_____

_____

_____

> **"Create in me a clean heart, O God, and renew a steadfast spirit within me."**
>
> **—King David Psalm 51:10**

Confession **DAY 20**

> **"I prayed to the Lord my God and confessed...."**
>
> **—Daniel Daniel 9:4**

Main Point to Remember from Day Nineteen:
If we don't confess, we will either hide our sin or blame others for it, but God still knows.

KEEPING OUR EYES ON GOD

To fully understand the principle of confession we must understand the principle of sin. We must acknowledge its origins. You see, without this recognition, we may be confessing the consequences of sin instead of the sin itself. In James 1:13–15, James writes, *"Let no one say when he is tempted, 'I am being tempted by God'; for God cannot be tempted by evil, and He Himself does not tempt anyone. But each one is tempted when he is carried away and enticed by his own lust. Then when lust has conceived, it gives birth to sin; and when sin is accomplished, it brings forth death."* In our confessions, we tend to focus on the action that is birthed or even the consequence that results, instead of focusing on the conception of it all. Sin begins in the heart, not in the actions. Our first sin is not the action of murder or adultery or stealing. It is being drawn away from God. When we allow our passion to leave God it will always find something else to attach itself to and that something will be something sinful. If our focus is on God, we will not see temptation. It is only when our eyes leave God that they find other things to attach themselves to.

Often, we are like Peter when he tried to walk on the water as Christ was doing. With his eyes on Jesus, he walked on the water. But when Jesus ceased to be Peter's focus, when his eyes shifted to the winds and the waves, worry and panic overwhelmed him, and he began to sink. (Actually, I think that for Peter to walk on water by focusing on Jesus is the greater miracle. God walking on water is awesome but to be expected—He is God. But a human walking on water is another thing altogether.)

Like Peter's, our focus on God is easily distracted by the winds and the waves of life's circumstances or the tempting lies of the enemy. As soon as this happens, we sink away from the victory that is ours in Christ and are enveloped in the waves. Whenever we lose our focus on God, we move in the direction of sin. It may be that we pursue worry, or that we pursue the solutions of self and striving, or that we run from the trial to the temporary pleasure of sin.

As you consider the principle of confession, consider this. One of the sins we frequently commit is the sin of not keeping focused on Him. Obedience is a reflection of faith. Disobedience is a reflection of unbelief—not believing what God says about the blessings of doing things His way or the consequences of choosing another way. All sin comes from the root of unbelief, and usually that lack of faith is a direct result of focusing on something other than God. Eve in the garden focused on the fruit instead of God's instruction. She listened to the serpent and entertained his calls to doubt. He drew her focus away from God to the false hope of supposed blessings outside the will of God. The serpent questioned the truth of God's words ("*You surely will not die!*" [Genesis 3:4]) and the goodness of His motives ("*God knows that in the day you eat from it your eyes will be opened, and you will be like God, knowing good and evil*" [Genesis 3:5]). In other words, the serpent was suggesting, "God is holding out on you—there is something good He doesn't want you to have." With Eve's focus on lies instead of truth, on Satan instead of God, sin was an easy step.

When we sin, we experience guilt. In our confession, however, we may focus on the symptom instead of the real problem. We may confess the action we committed that was wrong and miss the fact that the real sin happened earlier, when God ceased to be our focus. I should never be surprised at what sinful action shows up in my life when God is not my focus. Instead, I should be surprised that anything but sin ever shows up at that point. None of us keeps our eyes on God perfectly, but if we keep making the choice to put our eyes back on Him, we will experience His guiding and provision. He will also show us where we strayed, and that is what we need to confess—not just the results of turning from Him but the act of it as well.

FOR ME TO FOLLOW GOD
Write down the main idea that spoke to you personally from today's lesson.

_____

_____

_____

_____

_____

_____

_____

_____

ACTS PRAYING
"A"–ADORATION—In prayer, worship God for who He is and allow Him to capture your attention. Express your thoughts to God in the form of a written letter.

_____

_____

_____

_____

_____

_____

_____

_____

"Therefore, confess your sins to one another, and pray for one another so that you may be healed."

—James
James 5:16

"C"–CONFESSION—Confess any circumstances that are distracting you and anything else the Lord brings to mind. Again express your thoughts in writing.

_____

_____

_____

_____

_____

_____

_____

_____

"T"–THANKSGIVING—Thank God for His guidance, provision, and protection.

_____

_____

_____

_____

_____

_____

_____

_____

"S"–SUPPLICATION—Lift up to Him any needs or circumstances that are distracting you from seeing Him and trusting Him.

_____

_____

_____

_____

_____

_____

_____

_____

> *"I will go away and return to My place until they acknowledge their guilt and seek My face; in their affliction they will earnestly seek Me."*
>
> *—Jehovah*
> *Hosea 5:15*

Praying Scripture

The Lord, the Lord God, compassionate and gracious, slow to anger, and abounding in lovingkindness and truth; who keeps lovingkindness for thousands, who forgives iniquity, transgression and sin; yet He will by no means leave the guilty unpunished, visiting the iniquity of fathers on the children and on the grandchildren to the third and fourth generations. . . . If now I have found favor in Your sight, O Lord, I pray, let the Lord go along in our midst, even though the people are so obstinate, and pardon our iniquity and our sin, and take us as Your own possession. (Exodus 34:6–7, 9)

Main Point to Remember from Day Twenty:
The sins we need to confess are not just wrong actions, but also the leaving of God that made them possible.

THE LOVING FATHER WHO TAKES US BACK

Perhaps the most famous of all the stories Jesus told is the one we call the parable of the prodigal son, in Luke 15. It is familiar with good reason, because it paints a beautiful picture of coming back to God. In fact, some argue that it really should be called the parable of the loving father, since he is the central figure. But perhaps the reason we know it as the son's story is that we find such common ground with the prodigal son. Each of us is a prodigal child to God at some point. Each of us has gone our own way in selfishness. Each of us has experienced the tragic consequences of our rebellion, when we discover that sin isn't all it is cracked up to be. It takes us further than we thought we would stray; it keeps us longer than we thought we would stay; and it costs us more than we thought we would pay. But like the prodigal, we come to our senses. We repent of going our own way, remember what it was like in the Father's house, and return home. The beautiful part is, just as in this parable, God is waiting for us with the signet ring and the royal robe, ever ready to celebrate the penitent heart.

You may want to take the time to read the whole story. A prosperous man had two sons. One asked for his share of the family wealth and took off to have fun. Sin has pleasure for a season—if it didn't have some attraction, no one would do it. But sin's gratification is a *"passing pleasure"* (Hebrews 11:25). Unfortunately, just as the son's money was all spent, a famine hit the land, and the only work the lad could find was a job feeding pigs—the ultimate insult for a Jew, who considered swine unclean.

Sin has consequences, but that is not the greatest motivation for us to confess and repent. The greatest pull away from sin and back to God is the love of the Father. When we remember what it was like to be close to God, we recognize the value of what sin cost us. Psalm 16 warns us, *"The sorrows of those who have bartered for another god will be multiplied"* (verse 4), but it ends with this positive reminder: *"In Your presence is fullness of joy; in Your right hand there are pleasures forever"* (verse 11). The pleasure of the presence of God is not a passing one. What turned the prodigal son around was not just the consequences of his sin, but the memory of the Father's house:

> *"But when he came to his senses, he said, 'How many of my father's hired men have more than enough bread, but I am dying here with hunger! I will get up and go to my father, and will say to him, "Father, I have sinned against heaven, and in your sight; I am no longer worthy to be called your son; make me as one of your hired men.'"* (Luke 15:17–19)

The son did three things that give us a clear picture of what true confession is. First, he **remembered** what it was like to be close to the father. Second, he **recognized** what was wrong in his life. Third, he **returned**. That is what repentance is—turning from one thing and moving toward the opposite direction.

> **"Come, let us return to the Lord. For He has torn us, but He will heal us; He has wounded us, but He will bandage us."**
>
> **—Hosea**
> **Hosea 6:1**

The love of the father drew the son home. One more important point must be made, though. The son's planned speech to his father reveals a crucial mistake we all are in danger of making when we return to the Father. The son says, in essence, "Father, I'm no longer worthy to be a son, but will you take me back as a slave?" The question we must ask ourselves is, "Was he worthy before he left?" Even in a state of pharisaical obedience, the believer is not worthy of the Father's love. And if we believe that we must earn His favor instead of gratefully accepting it as an undeserved gift, then when we blow it (and we will), we will be slow to come back. We will wrongly view forgiveness as some spiritual form of probation—letting us slide so long as we keep our noses clean. The same flaw can be seen in the attitude of the other brother as well. He says, "Dad, I stayed, and you never gave me a party!" If we believe that we must earn God's love, then we will be proud and arrogant when we think we are behaving well, and when we are not we will wallow in our sin, doubting that we can be children of God again, or we will try to earn that position back by legalistic works. Which son do you identify with the most? Notice however, that the father doesn't let the prodigal finish his speech. God, who knows our hearts, will always take his children back when they repent and return, but He accepts us as family, not as slaves. His forgiveness is not probation.

FOR ME TO FOLLOW GOD

Write down the main idea that spoke to you personally from today's lesson.

_____

_____

_____

_____

_____

_____

_____

_____

_____

ACTS PRAYING

"A"–ADORATION—Take some time to praise God for who He is by identifying some of His attributes you find particularly meaningful and express these in a letter to Him. You may want to make use of a praise tape or some familiar choruses.

_____

_____

_____

_____

_____

_____

_____

_____

"I and my father's house have sinned. We have acted very corruptly against You and have not kept the commandments, nor the statutes, nor the ordinances which You commanded Your servant Moses."

—Nehemiah
Nehemiah 1:6b–7

"C"—CONFESSION—Remember, don't go looking for something to confess; instead, ask God to search your heart and bring to your mind anything that needs to be dealt with, especially in this area of returning to Him when you blow it.

_____
_____
_____
_____
_____
_____
_____
_____

"T"—THANKSGIVING—Thank God for the many blessings of your life, including His grace and His work in and through you, and take a moment to ask God what you need to be thankful for.

_____
_____
_____
_____
_____
_____
_____

"S"—SUPPLICATION—Pray for God to work in your life, showing you His will and helping you to do it. Bring to Him any requests and needs that are on your heart. Pray for any prodigals you know.

_____
_____
_____
_____
_____
_____
_____
_____

> **"Let Your ear now be attentive and Your eyes open to hear the prayer of Your servant which I am praying before You now, day and night, on behalf of the sons of Israel Your servants, confessing the sins of the sons of Israel which we have sinned against You."**
>
> **—Nehemiah**
> **Nehemiah 1:6**

Praying Scripture

O my God, incline Your ear and hear! Open Your eyes and see our desolations . . . for we are not presenting our supplications before You on account of any merits of our own, but on account of Your great compassion. O Lord, hear!

O Lord, forgive! O Lord, listen and take action! For Your own sake, O my God, do not delay, because . . . Your people are called by Your name. (Daniel 9:18–19)

Main Point to Remember from Day Twenty-One:
While sometimes the consequences of sin motivate us to confess and repent, often it is the love of the Father that makes us long to set things right with Him.

Main Ideas to Remember about the Principle of Confession:

❏ It is God's job to convict us of sin, but our job to respond with confession.

❏ Confession means to agree with God and is always accompanied by repentance.

❏ True confession requires humility and gives us practical access to God's grace.

❏ We are called to preserve the unity of the Spirit and must confess when we have not done that.

❏ If we don't confess, we will either hide our sin or blame others for it, but God still knows.

❏ The sins we need to confess are not just wrong actions, but also the leaving of God that made them possible.

❏ While sometimes the consequences of sin motivate us to confess and repent, often it is the love of the Father that makes us long to set things right with Him.

The Main Question to Ask Is . . .
Am I really agreeing with God about my sins?

"Remember me, O my God, for good."

—Nehemiah
Nehemiah 13:31

The Principle of Thanksgiving

Americans have set aside the fourth Thursday in November to observe the holiday we call Thanksgiving. We are supposed to use this day to remember our blessings with thankful hearts, but it is now an occasion known more for gorging than for gratitude. The Thanksgiving feast began as a celebration between the Pilgrims and their Native American friends, taking on a national character when President Lincoln formalized it during the Civil War. Although the official Thanksgiving holiday is a uniquely American observance, the practice of giving thanks is both universal and universally needed. It takes effort to remember and be grateful. The Russian novelist Fyodor Dostoevsky, writing about man, said, "If he is not stupid, he is monstrously ungrateful! Phenomenally ungrateful. In fact, I believe that the best definition of man is 'the ungrateful biped.'"[1]

Because we are prone to forget our past blessings, God had the nation of Israel establish memorial feasts throughout the year as annual reminders of what He had done for them. As New Covenant believers, we need to cultivate the habit of remembering, which can have a profound impact on our prayer life. First, giving thanks forces us to remember all that God has done before we ask Him to do more or complain of what He has not done for us. Second, taking time to be thankful for God's past

> *"Every gift I acknowledge reveals another and another until, finally, even the most normal, obvious and seemingly mundane event or encounter proves to be filled with grace."*
>
> **—Henri Nouwen**

faithfulness helps us trust Him with present needs. We are reminded of what He is able to do by reflecting on what He has already done. Taking time to remember has a profound influence on the attitudes of our hearts. Priest and writer Henri Nouwen has written, "Every gift I acknowledge reveals another and another until, finally, even the most normal, obvious and seemingly mundane event or encounter proves to be filled with grace" (*The Return of the Prodigal Son*, Doubleday, p. 86). Gratitude is not a gift that some possess. It is a habit that must be cultivated by all. G. K. Chesterton wrote, "You say grace before meals. All right. But I say grace before the concert and opera, and grace before sketching, painting, swimming, fencing, boxing, walking, playing, dancing, and grace before I dip the pen in ink" (as quoted on p. 77 of *Different Seasons: Twelve Months of Wisdom and Inspiration* by Dale Turner, High Tide Press, 1998).

God is the source of every blessing. Our Lord's brother wrote, *"Every good thing given and every perfect gift is from above, coming down from the Father of lights, with whom there is no variation or shifting shadow"* (James 1:17). In other words, if it is good, it came from God—and if it came from God, it is good. Yet often we do not take time to acknowledge what God has done for us. One of the key ingredients in spending time with God ought to be the practice of giving thanks. The great Christian thinker Os Guiness wrote, "Rebellion against God does not begin with the clenched fist of atheism but with the self-satisfied heart of the one for whom 'thank you' is redundant" (as quoted by Steve Cornell in his article *The True Reason for Thanksgiving*, available at http://www.songtime.com/sbc/sbc-thanks.htm). Thinking always precedes thankfulness, and when we spend time with the Lord, we need to take time to think and to thank.

THE ATTITUDE OF GRATITUDE

Consider this brief vignette of Jesus' travels from the Gospel of Luke:

> *While He was on the way to Jerusalem, He was passing between Samaria and Galilee. As He entered a village, ten leprous men who stood at a distance met Him; and they raised their voices, saying, "Jesus, Master, have mercy on us!" When He saw them, He said to them, "Go and show yourselves to the priests." And as they were going, they were cleansed. Now one of them, when he saw that he had been healed, turned back, glorifying God with a loud voice, and he fell on his face at His feet, giving thanks to Him. And he was a Samaritan. Then Jesus answered and said, "Were there not ten cleansed? But the nine—where are they? Was no one found who returned to give glory to God, except this foreigner?" And He said to him, "Stand up and go; your faith has made you well." (Luke 17:11–19.*

"[The Samaritan] fell on his face at His feet, giving thanks to Him."

Luke 17:16

Few today can relate to the suffering of those with the horrible disease called leprosy. This devastating scourge not only destroys its victims physically, but also robs them of all dignity and human interaction in the process. Lepers were outcasts in society in Jesus' day (as they are today, in parts of the world where the disease is still found)—they were to be avoided at all costs. We glimpse the pain of the lepers discussed by Luke in the fact that they stood at a distance. They dared not come close, but instead shouted their request from across the way: *"Jesus, Master, have mercy on us!"* I can't comprehend what joy and rapture they would have felt upon being healed. God had done a miracle; yet that really isn't the point of the story.

The key detail Luke wants us to grasp is the thankfulness of the one Samaritan. Wouldn't you know it! The nine Jews went their own way once they got what they wanted. But the Samaritan—the second-class citizen, a bi-racial person—was the only one who returned to thank the Lord for His mercy. *"But the nine—where are they?"* Jesus asks. I wonder how many times He has asked the same of us. How often have we been blessed by the Lord and forgotten our spiritual manners? How many gifts have arrived without gratitude? What supplications have been answered and then forgotten? It takes so little reflection to recognize how indebted we are to the Lord for his many kindnesses, yet we don't acknowledge them as we should.

The Jews looked down on the Samaritans, but in this man we find a model of how we ought to respond to the Lord's goodness. He glorified God *"with a loud voice."* Why is this significant? He was giving thanks to God, but not to God only. He wanted everyone to know what the Lord had done for him. He came to the Lord and fell at His feet. We think lightly of such physical humility, but this man didn't. Perhaps we feel awkward expressing overwhelming gratitude, but this only reveals how little we grasp all that has been done for us. This man was extravagant in giving thanks to the one who had done for him what only God could do. Every answered prayer is a miracle, but it is also an opportunity to thank the miracle giver. This man fell at Jesus' feet giving thanks for his healing.

God loves us. He invites us to cast our cares on Him because He cares for us. Isaiah 30:18 tells us, *"Therefore the Lord longs to be gracious to you, and therefore He waits on high to have compassion on you."* He doesn't need our gratitude, but He certainly deserves it. No, the need is on our part. We need to be grateful to insure that we do not forget His goodness or take it for granted. We need to give thanks to guard our hearts from selfishness. What have you to be thankful for?

FOR ME TO FOLLOW GOD

Write down the main idea that spoke to you personally from today's lesson.

_____

_____

_____

_____

_____

_____

_____

_____

_____

_____

_____

_____

> **"Was no one found who returned to give glory to God, except this foreigner?"**
>
> **—Jesus**
> **Luke 17:18**

ACTS PRAYING

"A"–ADORATION—Take some time to praise God for who He is by identifying some of His attributes you find particularly meaningful. Then express these in a letter to Him.

_____

_____

_____

_____

_____

_____

_____

_____

_____

"C"–CONFESSION—Don't go looking for something to confess; instead, ask God to search your heart and bring to your mind anything that needs to be dealt with.

_____

_____

_____

_____

_____

_____

_____

_____

_____

"T"–THANKSGIVING—Thank God for the many benefits of your walk with Him. Take a moment to ask Him to bring to your mind anything He has done for you that you haven't given thanks for.

_____

_____

_____

_____

_____

_____

_____

_____

_____

_____

"S"–SUPPLICATION—Pray for God to work in your life, and ask Him to make you aware of others you should be praying for.

_____
_____
_____
_____
_____
_____
_____
_____
_____

Praying Scripture

> *I will give thanks to the Lord with all my heart; I will tell of all Your wonders. I will be glad and exult in You; I will sing praise to Your name, O Most High (Psalm 9:1–2).*

Main Point to Remember from Day Twenty-Two:

We bring our concerns to the Lord, but it is easy to forget to thank Him for what He does for us.

> **"I will give thanks to the Lord according to His righteousness and will sing praise to the name of the Lord Most High."**
>
> **—King David**
> **Psalm 7:17**

GIVING THANKS FOR ALL THINGS

Thanksgiving **DAY 23**

Some years ago I was mowing the yard when the lawnmower struck a metal toy one of the children left in the yard. The blade struck the object and hurled it into the rear window of my car, shattering it into a million pieces. I was dumbfounded. I stopped the mower and just sat there staring at the damage. Quickly my shock turned to anger as I reflected on my child's carelessness and what it would cost me. But almost as fast, the Lord brought to my mind 1 Thessalonians 5:18, *"In everything give thanks; for this is God's will for you in Christ Jesus."* I know it had to be the Lord, because I certainly wasn't feeling thankful. "Lord, do You really want me to thank You for a broken windshield?" I thought. Yet the Scripture is clear—*"In everything give thanks. . . ."* Without much passion, and as an act of the will, I prayed, "I thank You Lord for my broken windshield," and He responded in my heart, "Aren't you glad you have a windshield to break?" I thanked Him for the car as I remembered what a blessing it had been when someone gave it to me. It had plenty of miles on it, but it got me to work without my wife having to take me and left our other car with her and the children.

It is amazing how thanking the Lord for one thing leads you to something else to be thankful for. My attitude began to change as I reflected on the blessing of the car. I thanked the Lord for the lawnmower. It was a used and beat-up riding mower I had bought from a neighbor, but it mowed the yard in an hour and a half instead of the four hours it took with the push mower. Then I thanked the Lord for the toy, and suddenly my heart was overwhelmed. The only reason I had the problem of that toy was that I had the

> **"In everything give thanks; for this is God's will for you in Christ Jesus."**
>
> **—The Apostle Paul I Thessalonians 5:18**

blessing of my children. I thought of all the families who want children and can't have them, and I thanked God that He blessed me with four. Then another thought hit me. What if that metal toy had struck one of my children instead of the car? I was flooded with thankfulness for things I hadn't even seen before. Yet what opened those floodgates was the choice to be obedient and give thanks for something I didn't feel thankful for.

Bing Crosby used to sing the song "Count Your Blessings." The whole song is a reminder of all we have to be thankful for, but one line in particular stands out to me. "When my bankroll is getting small, I think of when I had none at all, and I fall asleep counting my blessings." There is always something to be thankful for, yet often we rob ourselves of a thankful heart and withhold from God the gratitude He deserves, all because we focus on the wrong thing. We complain about what we have that we don't want, or we grumble about what we want that we don't have, and our vision is clouded so that we do not see all that God has done for us.

There are a few keys to remember as we reflect on 1 Thessalonians 5:18. First, this verse is a command, not a suggestion. The Greek verb translated *"give thanks," eucharisteo,* is an imperative and is in the present tense. We are commanded to continually give thanks. Second, there are no loopholes. We are ordered by God to give thanks *"in everything."* There is no getting around it. We are not called to feel thanks, but we are directed to give thanks. To do so is an act of faith. When we give thanks for something we don't feel thankful for, we are with our very words trusting God who allowed it into our lives and who is powerful enough to bring good out of it. *"In everything give thanks; for this is God's will for you in Christ Jesus."*

FOR ME TO FOLLOW GOD

Write down the main idea that spoke to you personally from today's lesson.

_____

_____

_____

_____

_____

_____

_____

_____

_____

_____

ACTS PRAYING

"A"–ADORATION—Take some time to worship God and to meditate on His attributes and power. Express these below in your letter to Him.

_____

_____

_____

_____

_____

_____
_____
_____
_____
_____
_____
_____

"C"–CONFESSION—Invite God to search your heart and bring to your mind anything that needs to be dealt with, especially in the area of giving thanks.

_____
_____
_____
_____
_____
_____
_____
_____
_____

"T"–THANKSGIVING—Today, make a choice to thank God for anything He brings to your mind that you don't currently feel thankful for.

_____
_____
_____
_____
_____
_____
_____
_____

"Always giving thanks for all things in the name of our Lord Jesus Christ to God, even the Father."

*—The Apostle Paul
Ephesians 5:20*

"S"–SUPPLICATION—Pray for God to work in your life, and ask Him to make you aware of others you should be praying for, especially those less fortunate than you.

_____
_____
_____
_____
_____
_____
_____
_____
_____

I will give thanks to You, O Lord, among the peoples; I will sing praises to You among the nations. For Your lovingkindness is great to the heavens and Your truth to the clouds. Be exalted above the heavens, O God; let Your glory be above all the earth. (Psalm 57:9–11)

Main Point to Remember from Day Twenty-Three:
We are commanded to give thanks in everything, not just those things we feel thankful for.

Thanksgiving **DAY 24**

> **God does not expect us to be thankful for tragedy. We shouldn't suppose that it is right or appropriate to welcome pain or to be grateful for it. But even though pain itself is not good, the results of it can be.**

GIVING THANKS FOR THE RESULTS

No matter how secure our environment or comfortable our situation, no immunization shots can protect us from trials. Each of us will encounter life head-on, with all its difficulties. Contrary to the teaching of some, Christianity is not a bridge over troubled water. Jesus said, *"In the world you have tribulation"* (John 16:33), and He said that so the disciples wouldn't be surprised when it happened. The joy of Christianity is not the absence of difficulties but the presence of God. In John 16:33, Jesus continues by saying, *"but take courage; I have overcome the world."* We have seen the call to give thanks in everything. But does that mean we are to be thankful for everything—even the hard things in our lives? God does not expect us to be thankful for tragedy. We shouldn't suppose that it is right or appropriate to welcome pain or to be grateful for it. But even though pain itself is not good, the results of it can be. A doctor's setting of a broken bone or stitching of a gaping wound has to cause pain, but the results achieved are positive, not negative.

The apostle Paul wrote to the Corinthian believers, *"Blessed be the God and Father of our Lord Jesus Christ, the Father of mercies and God of all comfort; who comforts us in all our affliction so that we will be able to comfort those who are in any affliction with the comfort with which we ourselves are comforted by God"* (2 Corinthians 1:3–4). What a joy in the midst of any distress to know the *"Father of mercies and God of all comfort."* As the psalmist said, *"I fear no evil, for You are with me"* (Psalm 23:4). It is during the difficult times that we are most keenly aware of the presence of God, and as we turn to Him we experience His comfort in all our afflictions. The reason is because of His great love and compassion for us—after all, He is the *"Father of mercies."* Although we may not be glad for the afflictions, we can be truly grateful for God's comfort in them. We come to know God and experience His presence when we go through trials in a way that would not be possible without them.

Not only is God's comfort abundant in all our afflictions, but there is a second blessing as well. With every gift of God's comfort that we receive, a door of ministry is opened up to us. He comforts us so that we may be comforted, but also so that we may be ministers of that comfort to those who are in any affliction. As we experience the comfort and power of God, He will lead us to others who need to experience it, also. Maybe they are going through a similar circumstance and need to hear what God has done for another. When my wife went through a battle with cancer, some of the people who ministered to us most were those who had been through a similar bout. Everything we experience in the way of trials purchases for us the right to be heard by those in similar trials. They want to hear what we have to say because they know we can truly relate. But even if we haven't gone through the same experiences as others and don't know how to comfort them, we know that we can still offer comfort. Paul tells us that when we have experienced God's comfort in the midst of our affliction, we are then able to *"comfort those who are in any affliction with the comfort with which we ourselves are comforted by God."* Even if we don't know exactly what they are going through, we do know the source of help—*"the Father of mercies and God of all comfort."*

When we think of the principle of thanksgiving, we are able to give thanks even for the difficult and tragic situations in our lives, because we know they enable us to experience God's comfort and equip us to bring that comfort to others.

FOR ME TO FOLLOW GOD

Write down the main idea that spoke to you personally from today's lesson.

_____

_____

_____

_____

_____

_____

_____

_____

_____

_____

_____

_____

_____

ACTS PRAYING

"A"–ADORATION—This passage tells us that the God who has blessed us with comfort Himself deserves to be blessed (to be adored and thanked for all benefits). Take some time to do this in your letter to Him.

_____

_____

_____

_____

_____

_____

_____

_____

_____

_____

_____

_____

"C"–CONFESSION—Don't go looking for something to confess; just ask God to bring to your mind anything that needs to be dealt with.

_____

_____

_____

_____

_____

_____

_____

_____

_____

_____

"T"–THANKSGIVING—Thank God for His supernatural comfort in the midst of your circumstances. Thank Him for comfort you have received in the past, and by faith thank Him for comfort you presently need.

_____

_____

_____

_____

_____

_____

_____

_____

_____

_____

"S"–SUPPLICATION—Pray for those you know who need God's comfort and for Him to lead you to those you can comfort because of what God has done for you.

_____

_____

_____

_____

_____

_____

_____

_____

_____

"O, give thanks to the Lord, for He is good; for His lovingkindness is everlasting."

—David
1 Chronicles 16:34

Save us, O God of our salvation, and gather us and deliver us from the nations, to give thanks to Your holy name, and glory in Your praise. Blessed be the Lord, the God of Israel, from everlasting even to everlasting. (1 Chronicles 16:35–36a)

Main Point to Remember from Day Twenty-Four:
God does not expect us to be thankful for tragedy, but we can be thankful for the positive results He brings from it.

GIVING THANKS FOR THE PEOPLE IN OUR LIVES

Thanksgiving **DAY 25**

Solomon, history's wisest and wealthiest king, compiled a collection of wise sayings that we call the book of Proverbs. When he took the throne, God invited him to ask for anything, and instead of asking for riches he asked for wisdom. God honored that request and blessed us all through his words. One of the most intriguing of Solomon's sayings that I have found is Proverbs 14:4, *"Where no oxen are, the manger is clean, but much revenue comes by the strength of the ox."* I'm sure many would look at this verse and wonder what it has to do with anything, but hidden in this obscure nugget of proverbial wisdom is a powerful principle that applies to many different areas of our walk with God. Try to think with the mind of a farmer. The farmer who has no ox in his stable has no manure to clean up, but he has no milk, either, and when he needs to plow his fields or haul a heavy burden, he must do so alone. If he wants the added benefits that owning an ox offers, he must accept the problems and responsibilities that come with it.

The parallel to other areas of life is striking. Too often we choose the path of least resistance. We seek to avoid pain and problems, yet in the process we rob ourselves of opportunities for growth and benefit. The locker room adage "no pain, no gain" holds true for more than just weight lifting. If we choose not to open up and share ourselves with others, we don't experience the pain and problems that relationships can bring, but we also don't experience the joys and growth.

Many times we purchase an "ox" (by entering into a relationship with someone or making a commitment to something) and then naively expect that there will be no problems with it. When the problems or difficulties come (as they always do), we balk, as if something were terribly wrong. Sometimes we bail out when we shouldn't, all because, figuratively speaking, we don't like the smell of manure, or don't know how to use a relationship "shovel." In the process we rob ourselves of the benefits that come *"by the strength of the ox."* Often our relationships are not appreciated as they should be, or sometimes they are even avoided because we focus on the troubles and responsibilities instead of the benefits and blessings. Sometimes we find ourselves wishing certain people weren't in our lives instead of being thankful for them, yet *"much revenue"* comes to our lives from their sovereignly appointed presence. God wants us to be thankful for the people He places in our lives. Paul wrote to the Thessalonians, *"We give thanks to God always for all of you, making mention of you in our prayers"* (1 Thessalonians 1:2). God desires that we have this same attitude toward everyone in our lives, even the unlovely. The difficult people and challenging relationships in our lives teach us how to love others with grace, as the Lord loves us.

> **"Through Him then, let us continually offer up a sacrifice of praise to God, that is, the fruit of lips that give thanks to His name."**
>
> **—The Unknown Writer of Hebrews Hebrews 13:15**

> "We give thanks to God always for all of you, making mention of you in our prayers."
>
> —The Apostle Paul
> 1 Thessalonians 1:2

Have you ever thanked the Lord for the people in your life? There are probably many whom you appreciate greatly but have never thanked the Lord for bringing to you. There may be others whom you are unthankful for and wish you could avoid. It may be because you have focused on the manure of the relationship, which has caused you to miss the milk. Take some time today to thank the Lord for the people in your life.

FOR ME TO FOLLOW GOD

Write down the main idea that spoke to you personally from today's lesson.

_____

_____

_____

_____

_____

_____

_____

ACTS PRAYING

"A"–ADORATION—Take some time to praise God for who He is by identifying some of His attributes that you find particularly meaningful. Then express these in a letter to Him.

_____

_____

_____

_____

_____

_____

_____

_____

"C"–CONFESSION—Don't go looking for something to confess; instead, ask God to search your heart and bring to your mind anything that needs to be dealt with. Be sensitive to any attitudes toward people that have been wrong.

_____

_____

_____

_____

_____

_____

_____

"T"–THANKSGIVING—Thank God for the many benefits of your walk with Him and for the joy of the people in your life. Take a moment to ask God what (and whom) you need to be thankful for.

_____
_____
_____
_____
_____
_____
_____
_____
_____
_____
_____

"S"–SUPPLICATION—Pray for God's wisdom in the choices of life, and ask God to make you aware of others for whom you should be praying.

_____
_____
_____
_____
_____
_____
_____
_____
_____
_____

Praying Scripture

Blessed are You, O Lord God of Israel our father, forever and ever. Yours, O Lord, is the greatness and the power and the glory and the victory and the majesty, indeed everything that is in the heavens and the earth; Yours is the dominion, O Lord, and You exalt Yourself as head over all. Both riches and honor come from You, and You rule over all, and in Your hand is power and might; and it lies in Your hand to make great and to strengthen everyone. Now therefore, our God, we thank You, and praise Your glorious name. (1 Chronicles 29:10b–13)

Main Point to Remember from Day Twenty-Five:
We need to be thankful for the people in our lives, even the relationships that are challenging.

> **"At that very moment she came up and began giving thanks to God, and continued to speak of Him to all those who were looking for the redemption of Jerusalem."**
>
> **—Luke's description of Anna, the Prophetess, who spoke in the Temple regarding the birth of Jesus**
> **Luke 2:38**

RECOGNIZING AND GIVING THANKS FOR WHAT WE ALREADY HAVE

The apostle Paul begins his letter to the Ephesian believers with an interesting invitation. He is passionate for these believers that he has helped to nurture in the faith. He has goals and ambitions for how they will live, and he longs to see them *"walk in a manner worthy"* of their calling. But he doesn't start by telling them what they need to do. Instead, he spends the first half of the epistle instructing them in what they need to remember. He launches his exhortation with an invitation to praise and thanksgiving. In Ephesians 1:3, He invites them to bless the Lord: *"Blessed be the God and Father of our Lord Jesus Christ, who has blessed us with every spiritual blessing in the heavenly places in Christ."* Think about that. What he is telling the Ephesians (and us) is that we have already been blessed with everything in Jesus.

In Texas, in the "land west of the Pecos River," there is a famous oil field known as Yates Field. During the early 1900s, this land was owned by a rancher named Thomas Hickox. In early 1915, Hickox was eager to unload this seemingly desolate expanse of land and made an offer to trade the 16,640-acre plot to Ira Yates for a small dry goods store that Yates owned. At the time, those familiar with the proposed trade thought Hickox was getting the better end of the deal. In fact, friends advised Yates against bartering away his profitable store, claiming that "even Buffalo know better than to cross the Pecos" and that "a crow would not fly over it," and that the land was not worth the taxes. Yet Yates and Hickox went ahead with the trade anyway, and for several years, Yates struggled to make the ranch profitable. [2]

In the early 1920s, oil was being discovered in various places throughout West Texas, but geologists did not believe that any oil would be found west of the Pecos. However, Ira Yates, stricken with "the oil fever" was able to persuade a reluctant Levi Smith of the Transcontinental Oil Company to drill on his ranch, despite its desolate location. On October 28, 1926, Yates became an instant millionaire when the drilling crews struck oil for the very first time. [3] The crews were about to discover one of the largest oil resevoirs in the entire world. Nearly eighty years later, the Yates Field is second only to the Prudhoe Bay, Alaska, oil field in terms of estimated oil reserves known to exist in the United States. [4]

The peculiar angle to this true story is that Thomas Hickox traded this bountiful tract of land in 1915 to Ira Yates for a rickety, old dry goods store. What on earth was Hickox thinking? He simply had no idea that he was sitting on one of the richest oil fields ever to be found. He owned it, but he never possessed it, because he was unaware of the wealth that already belonged to him.

It seems so odd that a man sitting on land worth billions would trade it all away for a country store. Yet often we come to God without ever acknowledging or even remembering what we already possess in Christ. We are ignorant of the wealth we already have because we have not investigated what lies beneath the surface. Like Mr. Hickox and even Mr. Yates before the oil was discovered, many Christians live in ignorance of their vast riches, unaware of how blessed they are in Christ.

"Give thanks to the Lord, call on His name. Make known His deeds among the peoples; make them remember that His name is exalted. Praise the Lord in song, for He has done excellent things; let this be known throughout the earth."

Isaiah 12:4–5

Practically speaking, we can divide most Christians into two camps: those who are trying to get things from Christ, and those who realize that they already have all things in Christ. As Paul put it in Romans 8:32, *"He who did not spare His own Son, but delivered Him over for us all, how will He not also with Him freely give us all things?"* One of the blessings and responsibilities of the principle of thanksgiving is that it draws our focus away from what we perceive as our need and places it on what we already have. Often, in the process, we discover that we already have what we need but have not laid hold of it by faith. Or we have not accessed it, because we are enamored of earthly trinkets unworthy to be compared with it. We need to be students of what is already ours, and we must remember to be thankful for those blessings.

FOR ME TO FOLLOW GOD

1. As you consider today's truth, is there some specific area you are aware of in which you need to grow?

_____

_____

_____

_____

_____

_____

_____

2. Why not take a few moments to jot down some of the many riches God has given each of us through Christ, as listed in Ephesians 1:3–14?

_____

_____

_____

_____

_____

_____

_____

ACTS PRAYING

"A"–ADORATION—Take some time to praise God for who He is by identifying some of His attributes that you find particularly meaningful. Then express these attributes in a letter to Him. A good passage to meditate on today is Psalm 100.

_____

_____

_____

_____

_____

_____

"In God we have boasted all day long, and we will give thanks to Your name forever."

—The Sons of Korah
Psalm 44:8

"We give thanks to You, O God, we give thanks, For Your name is near."

—Asaph, David's chief musician
Psalm 75:1

"C"–CONFESSION—Don't go looking for something to confess; instead, ask God to search your heart and bring to your mind anything that needs to be dealt with.

_____

_____

_____

_____

_____

_____

_____

_____

_____

"T"–THANKSGIVING—Thank God for the many blessings of your life, taking a moment to ask God what you need to be thankful for. Thank Him for the many blessings that are yours in Christ, as you read in Ephesians 1:3–14.

_____

_____

_____

_____

_____

_____

_____

"S"–SUPPLICATION—Pray for God to work in your life by helping you to be more aware of who you are in Christ. And ask Him to make you aware of areas in which you need to grow and truths that you need to know and apply.

_____

_____

_____

_____

_____

_____

_____

_____

"It is good to give thanks to the Lord and to sing praises to Your name, O Most High; To declare Your lovingkindness in the morning and Your faithfulness by night, . . . for You, O Lord, have made me glad by what You have done, I will sing for joy at the works of Your hands."

—a song for the Sabbath day Psalm 92:1–2, 4

We give thanks to You, O God, we give thanks, for Your name is near; [we] declare Your wondrous works. . . . As for me, I will declare it forever; I will sing praises to the God of Jacob. (Psalm 75:1, 9)

Main Point to Remember from Day Twenty-Six:
We need to be aware of what we already have and take time to be thankful for it.

GIVING THANKS FOR THE RIGHT THINGS

Thanksgiving **DAY 27**

Are you thankful for the right things? This is a question that demands reflection. We ought to be thankful for our blessings, and we may be truly thankful for those things we have identified as blessings, but it is possible to be thankful for the wrong things. The prodigal son was thankful when his father agreed to give him his inheritance early. But was this really a blessing? Later he would reckon that abundance as a curse, for it only fed the flames of excess in his habits. Judas probably was thankful for the thirty pieces of silver he received for betraying Jesus, but in the end the money was used to purchase his burial plot. Satan was probably thankful beyond his wildest dreams when Jesus was nailed to the cross but did not even recognize that what he had wished for sealed his own doom.

You see, if our hearts are selfish, we will be thankful for things that please our flesh, not recognizing that what gives pleasure in the short run may end in pain. We ought to be thankful, but we must be sure that we are thankful for the right things. In the end, we may discover that some of the things we wish to avoid are blessings in disguise.

The apostle Paul wrote to the Colossian believers, *"We give thanks to God, ... since we heard of your faith in Christ Jesus and the love which you have for all the saints; because of the hope laid up for you in heaven. . . . "* (Colossians 1:3–5). He thanked the Lord for them, but in the process, he recognized the right things to be thankful for. He thanked God for three things—their faith, their love, and their hope. Why did he select those things to be thankful for? Obviously, we trust that Paul wrote under the inspiration of the Holy Spirit. Therefore we can trust that he was thankful for the right things.

You can learn the right things to be thankful for by paying attention to what the Bible writers commended or condemned in those to whom they wrote. As you do this, a pattern quickly emerges. In 1 Corinthians 13:13 Paul writes, *"But now [abide] faith, hope, love. . . . "* Why did he select only these three? As we look at the books of the New Testament, we find this trio or some of these three mentioned in almost every letter. Usually they appear as issues either of commendation or condemnation for those to whom they are directed. In the letter to the believers at Colossae, we see all three listed as compliments. That ought to tell us something about what God considers important in our relationship with Him.

The epistles clearly show that the three essential areas of growth are faith, hope, and love. Faith—the strength of our ability to trust God—is like a muscle that grows with use. The more we trust God, the more we are able

"We give thanks to God. . . . because of the hope laid up for you in heaven."

—The Apostle Paul Colossians 1:3, 5

to trust Him. Without faith, it is impossible to please God (Hebrews 11:6). Hope is what keeps us going and keeps us from entangling ourselves in this present life. It is our hope that helps us to look beyond the temporal day-to-day issues to see the eternal ones. Another description for hope is "eternal perspective"—what keeps our values aligned with God's. And love is our ultimate calling. The *"great commandment"* is to *"love the Lord your God with all your heart, and with all your soul, and with all your mind."* And the second commandment (which, in Jesus' words, "is like it") is to *"love your neighbor as yourself"* (Matthew 22:37, 39). How we are doing in loving God and loving others says a lot about how healthy our walk with Christ is.

If Paul were writing a letter to you, what would he say about your faith, hope, and love? If we want to be all that God wants us to be, we must regularly monitor how we are doing in these three key areas. To be thankful for the right things means that we are thankful for those things that help us in faith, hope, and love. I may wish that I could avoid trials, but they make my faith grow. I may not be grateful for tragedy—especially the loss of someone I love—but tragic events shape my hope and make me long for heaven. I must learn to be thankful for those situations and people that God uses to teach me to love.

FOR ME TO FOLLOW GOD

Write down the main idea that spoke to you personally from today's lesson.

_____

_____

_____

_____

_____

_____

_____

_____

_____

ACTS PRAYING

"A"–ADORATION—Take some time to praise God for who He is by identifying some of His attributes that you find particularly meaningful. Then express these in a letter to Him.

_____

_____

_____

_____

_____

_____

_____

_____

"C"–CONFESSION—Remember, don't go looking for something to confess; instead, ask God to search your heart and bring to your mind anything that needs to be dealt, with especially in the key areas of faith, hope, and love.

_____

_____

_____

_____

_____

_____

_____

_____

_____

"T"–THANKSGIVING—Thank God for the many blessings of your life, taking a moment to ask Him if there is something you haven't been thankful for that you should be, or if there are any areas in which you have been thankful for the wrong things.

_____

_____

_____

_____

_____

_____

_____

_____

"O Lord, You are my God; I will exalt You, I will give thanks to Your name; for You have worked wonders, plans formed long ago, with perfect faithfulness."

—Isaiah

Isaiah 25:1

"S"–SUPPLICATION—Pray for God to work in your life, building your faith, hope, and love, and then pray this for those whom you hold dear. Bring to Him any requests and needs that are on your heart.

_____

_____

_____

_____

_____

_____

_____

_____

Praying Scripture

Blessed be the Lord God, the God of Israel, Who alone works wonders. And blessed be His glorious name forever; and may the whole earth be filled with His glory. Amen, and Amen. (Psalm 72:18–19).

Main Point to Remember from Day Twenty-Seven:
We need to make sure that we are thankful for the right things.

Thanksgiving **DAY 28**

> *"It is You who has kept my soul from the pit of nothingness, for You have cast all my sins behind Your back. For Sheol cannot thank You, death cannot praise You; those who go down to the pit cannot hope for Your faithfulness. It is the living who give thanks to You, as I do today; a father tells his sons about Your faithfulness."*
>
> **—King Hezekiah
> Isaiah 38:17–19**

BLESSING THE LORD

Do you know what it means to "bless the Lord"? The Hebrew word for "bless" has the idea of adoring and thanking God for all benefits. In Psalm 103, David exclaims, "Bless the Lord, O my soul, and all that is within me, bless His holy name. Bless the Lord, O my soul, and forget none of His benefits" (Psalm 103:1–2). The interesting thing here is not just what is said, but also to whom it is spoken. David is talking to himself. He is carrying on a conversation with his own soul, commanding his soul to "bless the Lord." What we see here is the role of the will in thanksgiving. Although a thankful heart can be flooded with emotion and passion, if we wait until we feel like it, we won't be thankful as often as we should. The reason for this is simple—thinking precedes thankfulness. The emotions and feelings of thankfulness are the result of the choice, not the reason for it. David commands his soul to bless the Lord and then instructs himself in how to do it. When he begins this dialogue with his inner being, David calls for "all that is within" himself to respond. There is no such thing as half-hearted thankfulness. We are either grateful or ungrateful.

More important, David coaches his soul to *"forget none of His benefits."* This is the key to thankfulness. Thinking comes first. The inner being is woefully forgetful. It is easily distracted from past blessings by focusing on present challenges. We must, by choice, remind ourselves of the things God has done for us.

In David's internal conversation, his mind immediately moves to five benefits that he recognizes of what God has done for him. At the top of the list is forgiveness: he reminds his soul that it is the Lord *"who pardons all . . . iniquities"* (verse 3). Our greatest need—the forgiveness of our sins—is God's greatest gift to us. If He never did another thing for us during the rest of our lives, He would be worthy of eternal thanks for that one act alone. But forgiveness is just the beginning of His benefits to us. David continues in verse 3 by reminding his soul to bless the Lord because He *"heals all . . . diseases."* God can and does heal us temporally, but we must remember that the ultimate healing will come when He gives us glorified bodies that have no stain of sin or sickness and will never grow old. In verse 4, David brings up another blessing, telling his soul that God *"redeems your life from the pit."* The Hebrew word for "pit" means "ruin," "destruction," or "corruption." This speaks not just of forgiveness but also of deliverance. God not only forgives our sins but delivers us from their control. (If you ever have trouble being thankful, try to remember where your life would be if He hadn't redeemed it.)

Verse 4 continues by saying that God is the One who *"crowns you with lovingkindness and compassion."* His steadfast, loyal love and His compassion for all our trials and troubles are as a victor's wreath around our heads. The word "crowns" literally means "to encircle": He has surrounded us with His love and care. Finally, David reminds himself that it is God *"who satisfies your years with good things, so that your youth is renewed like the eagle."* God alone gives us those good things of the soul. This last benefit is the culmination of everything else He has done for us. Thank You, Lord!

The rest of Psalm 103 is a celebration of the benefits of knowing God. We are reminded that He *"performs righteous deeds"* (verse 6) and that He reveals Himself to us (verse 7). Our memory is brought back to what He is like— *"compassionate and gracious, slow to anger and abounding in lovingkindness"* (verse 8). David also rehearses for us what God has not done: *"He has not dealt with us according to our sins, nor rewarded us according to our iniquities"* (verse 10). David reminds himself (and us) of all that God promises to do, as well. He will love us faithfully (verse 11), forgive us completely (verse 12), care for us deeply (verse 13), know us fully (verse 14), and commit to us permanently (verse 17).

Join with King David, and tell your soul to bless the Lord.

FOR ME TO FOLLOW GOD
Write down the main idea that spoke to you personally from today's lesson.

_____

_____

_____

_____

_____

_____

_____

ACTS PRAYING
"A"–ADORATION—Take some time to praise God for who He is by identifying some of His attributes that you find particularly meaningful. Then express these in a letter to Him.

_____

_____

_____

_____

_____

_____

_____

_____

_____

"Yet again there will be heard in this place . . . in the cities of Judah and in the streets of Jerusalem . . . the voice of joy and the voice of gladness, the voice of the bridegroom and the voice of the bride, the voice of those who say, 'Give thanks to the Lord of hosts, for the Lord is good, For His lovingkindness is everlasting.' "

—Jeremiah Jeremiah 33:10–11

"Now when Daniel knew that the document was signed, he entered his house (now in his roof chamber he had windows open toward Jerusalem); and he continued kneeling on his knees three times a day, praying and giving thanks before his God, as he had been doing previously."

—Daniel 6:10

"C"–CONFESSION—Don't focus on yourself. Instead, focus on the Lord and all His benefits. As you gaze on Him, be willing to quickly confess and turn from anything that God reveals is separating you from Him.

_____

_____

_____

_____

_____

_____

_____

_____

_____

"T"–THANKSGIVING—*"Forget none of His benefits."* Don't just think about being thankful. Make use of Psalm 103 and verbalize to the Lord how grateful you are for everything this wonderful psalm brings to your mind.

_____

_____

_____

_____

_____

_____

_____

_____

"S"–SUPPLICATION—Bring to God any needs for yourself and others in your life. At the same time, make sure you ask for His help in having a thankful heart.

_____

_____

_____

_____

_____

_____

_____

_____

_____

Praying Scripture

Lord [You have] established [Your] throne in the heavens, and [Your] sovereignty rules over all. Bless the Lord, you His angels, mighty in strength, who perform His word, obeying the voice of His word! Bless the Lord, all you His hosts, you who serve Him, doing His will. Bless the Lord, all you works of His, in all places of His dominion; Bless the Lord, O my soul! (Psalm 103:19–22)

Main Point to Remember from Day Twenty-Eight:

Thinking must come first if we are to be thankful.

Main Ideas to Remember about the Principle of Thanksgiving:

☐ We bring our concerns to the Lord, but it is easy to forget to thank Him for what He does for us.

☐ We are commanded to give thanks in everything, not just those things we feel thankful for.

☐ God does not expect us to be thankful for tragedy, but we can be thankful for the positive results He brings from it.

☐ We need to be thankful for the people in our lives, even the relationships that are challenging.

☐ We need to be aware of what we already have and take time to be thankful for it.

☐ We need to make sure that we are thankful for the right things.

☐ Thinking must come first if we are to be thankful.

The Main Question to Ask Is . . .

Am I truly thankful for all that God has done for me?

> **"They sang, praising and giving thanks to the Lord, saying, 'For He is good, for His lovingkindness is upon Israel forever.'"**
>
> **Ezra 3:11**

Notes

1. *Notes from the Underground,* 1913 translation by C. J. Hogarth (Great Classics Library) (Longmeadow Press), 613.

2. *TSHA Online: A Digital Gateway to Texas History at the University of Texas at Austin,* http://www.tsha.utexas.edu/handbook/online/articles/view/YY/fyazp.html/.

3. *Ibid.*

4. *Wanderings Around the Patch.* "Queen of the Pecos: Discovery of the Yates Oilfield in West Texas," http://www.0.drillinginfo.com/community/wanderings/wonderings20020101.htm/.

Notes

THE PRINCIPLE OF SCRIPTURE

*T*he goal of the Christian life is to be a faithful disciple or follower of Jesus. Our Lord says in John 15:7, *"If you abide in Me, and My words abide in you, ask whatever you wish, and it will be done for you."* Time with God must include time in His Word. Our prayer life is built on the foundation of an abiding relationship with Christ and regular immersion in His words. This week we look at the principle of Scripture and its role in the quiet time.

The Word of God stands as the most unique book in history. It was written over a period of thousands of years by some forty different authors from all walks of life: kings and shepherds, fishermen and farmers. And yet its theme is incredibly consistent, as we look at its sixty-six different books. How could men from different times, different places, different cultures, and different occupations weave together such sublime words of wisdom? Peter explains: *"But know this first of all, that no prophecy of Scripture is a matter of one's own interpretation, for no prophecy was ever made by an act of human will, but men moved by the Holy Spirit spoke from God"* (2 Peter 1:20–21). Though He used many different people as His instruments in writing it, God is the author of the Bible. It is His work and His words.

> *"If you abide in Me, and My words abide in you, ask whatever you wish, and it will be done for you."*
>
> **—Jesus**
> **John 15:7**

Imagine that you are standing on the shore of a beautiful, deserted beach in the Caribbean. You look out over the pristine, clear water and think, "How beautiful!" Now imagine that you put on a snorkel mask and dive in. The surface of the Caribbean Sea is beautiful, but once you dive beneath the surface you find it is more beautiful still. You discover that there is much more to be seen than just the water and the waves, such as the incredible diversity of aquatic life, with so many different shapes and colors and the majestic beauty of coral reefs that took generations to take shape. The Word of God is like that. You read it and see its beauty, but the more you study it, the more beauty you discover. Every day of our lives we have the opportunity to see something new in the Word of God.

It is amazing to realize that God has written a book. Think of how important an issue that is in faith. It is yet another way that God has stooped to communicate Himself in a way that we can understand. John Wesley (founder of the Methodist Church), in the preface to his *Standard Sermons,* wrote:

> *I am a creature of a day, passing through life as an arrow through the air. I am a spirit coming from God and returning to God, hovering over the great gulf. A few months hence I am no more seen. I drop into an unchangeable eternity. I want to know one thing—if God Himself has condescended to teach the way. He hath written it down in a book. . . . Oh, give me that book! At any price, give me the book of God!*

Is it your passion to read God's Word, as it was John Wesley's? It should be!

Scripture   **DAY 29**

WHAT GOD'S WORD WILL DO IN OUR LIVES

It truly is an amazing thought that God has chosen to reveal Himself. Even though He tells us, *"As the heavens are higher than the earth, so are My ways higher than your ways and My thoughts than your thoughts"* (Isaiah 55:9), God has stooped from the heights to disclose Himself to humankind. He has revealed Himself in creation to the point that *"His invisible attributes, His eternal power and divine nature, have been clearly seen, being understood through what has been made"* (Romans 1:20). But His revelation does not stop there. Listen to what David writes in Psalm 19. He begins in verse 1 by instructing us, *"The heavens are telling of the glory of God; and their expanse is declaring the work of His hands."* But then David shows us how God has disclosed Himself in a more specific way—that He has communicated Himself even more clearly through the Scriptures. Psalm 19 continues,

> *The law of the Lord is perfect, restoring the soul; the testimony of the Lord is sure, making wise the simple. The precepts of the Lord are right, rejoicing the heart; the commandment of the Lord is pure, enlightening the eyes. The fear of the Lord is clean, enduring forever; the judgments of the Lord are true; they are righteous altogether. They are more desirable than gold, yes, than much fine gold; sweeter also than honey and the drippings of the honeycomb. Moreover, by them Your servant is warned; in keeping them there is great reward. (Psalm 19:7–11)*

Psalm 19 paints a pretty awesome portrait of the Word of God. Look at the terms it uses to describe the nature of Scripture. God's law is *"perfect"*—it is flawless and free from blemish. The Lord's testimony is sure—firm and able to support us. His precepts are *"right"*—they are straight and upright. God's commandment is *"pure"*—unstained and without error. It is *"clean"*—unalloyed, according to the Hebrew word used here. Nothing else is mixed in. The judgments are the Lord are *"true"*—the Hebrew word speaks of firmness and stability. God's truths are *"more desirable than gold"* and *"sweeter than honey."* These statements are all focused on what God's Word is like. But we also find revealed here a list of all that the Word of God is able to do in our lives.

What is the need of your life right now? Is your inner being damaged and fractured and in turmoil? The Scriptures can restore your soul—your inner self—your mind, will, and emotions. Do you lack wisdom for the challenges of life? They can make wise the simple-minded. Do you need encouragement? They can give joy to the heart. Need direction? God's Word can enlighten your way. These truths of God that we call the Bible last forever and are altogether righteous. They warn us of danger but also point us toward reward as we obey what they say. The Scriptures can help us to discern error and guard us from sinning intentionally. The Bible is able to work in our hearts so that our words and thoughts become pleasing to God. What a book is this book of books!

Whatever you need, the Word offers. If you need wisdom or restoration, joy or enlightenment—even if you need warning, the Word is able to do that. In 1 Thessalonians 2:13, the apostle Paul speaks of the Scriptures as *"the word of God, which also performs its work in you who believe."* For us to have the benefits of the Word, though, we must know what it says, and we must unite what we read with faith. It performs its work *"in you who believe."*

FOR ME TO FOLLOW GOD

Write down the main idea that spoke to you personally from today's lesson.

_____

_____

_____

_____

_____

_____

_____

ACTS PRAYING

"A"–ADORATION—Take some time to praise God for who He is by identifying some of His attributes that you find particularly meaningful. Then express these attributes in your letter to Him. A good passage to meditate on today is Psalm 19.

_____

_____

_____

_____

_____

_____

_____

> In 1 Thessalonians 2:13, the apostle Paul speaks of the Scriptures as "the word of God, which also performs its work in you who believe."

"C"–CONFESSION—Remember, don't go looking for something to confess; instead, ask God to search your heart and bring to your mind anything that needs to be dealt with.

_____

_____

_____

_____

_____

_____

_____

_____

"How can a young man keep his way pure? By keeping it according to Your word."

—Psalm 119:9

"T"–THANKSGIVING—Thank God for the many benefits of your walk with Him and for the joy of knowing Him and experiencing the abundant life He gives. Thank Him for His Word and all that it offers you. What else do you need to be thankful for today?

_____

_____

_____

_____

_____

_____

_____

_____

"Your word I have treasured in my heart, that I may not sin against You."

—Psalm 119:11

"S"–SUPPLICATION—Pray for God to work in your life in a compelling way, and ask God to make you aware of others for whom you should be praying.

_____

_____

_____

_____

_____

_____

_____

_____

Deal bountifully with Your servant, that I may live and keep Your word. Open my eyes, that I may behold wonderful things from Your law (Psalm 119:17–18).

Main Point to Remember from Day Twenty-Nine:
God's Word performs a work in our lives when we believe.

The Power of Reading the Word

Scripture **DAY 30**

One of the most incredible realities of the Word of God is that it speaks afresh every time we read it. We need to be reminded even of those truths that we understand, because our call is not simply to understand truth but also to live it. The great evangelist D. L. Moody put it this way: "The only way to keep a broken vessel full is to keep the faucet running."[1] This is why we need to read and study God's Word over and over. But, in practical terms, how do we do that? How do we let His words abide in us? The rest of this lesson is devoted to practical ways that we can fulfill this part of being a disciple.

For the words of Jesus to abide in us, we must spend much time with them. The term "abide" has the idea of being at home. Colossians 3:16 tells us, *"Let the word of Christ richly dwell within you."* It goes on to explain that when Christ dwells in us, we will teach and admonish others with wisdom. But does this mean that we must all go to seminary and learn to read and speak Greek and Hebrew? Many people wrongly believe that Bible study, like something we see a stunt driver do on television, needs the disclaimer, "Don't try this at home." We fear that, to really understand the Bible, one must be an "ivory tower" intellectual or a member of a religious order hidden away behind ancient stone walls. Well, maybe an intellectual or a devout monk can get a lot out of the Scriptures, but so can you. Remember, we saw in Psalm 19:7 that God's word can *"make wise the simple."* The Bible is an inexhaustible source of wisdom and knowledge. The more we study it, the more we can learn. But it reaches down to right where we are. Studying the Bible doesn't begin with parsing Greek verbs found in dusty textbooks; it begins simply by reading.

During the reign of King Josiah, a great revival came to the people of Judah. Josiah's father Amon and his grandfather Manasseh had led God's people astray, into idol worship. The temple of God had fallen into disrepair. But Josiah became a reformer. Through his leadership and the godly influence of believers around him, the Temple was cleaned up and repaired. In the process, someone discovered a copy of the Scriptures. So neglected was the spiritual life of the nation that no one even knew what the Bible said. In 2 Chronicles 34:14–21, we see the impact that hearing the Word of God had on King Josiah. He and the people of Judah did not have evil in their hearts, yet their lives were not what they should have been. Once the Word of God was read, Josiah fell under conviction. He recognized things that were wrong in the nation; he saw their sin. He tore his robes—a sign in his culture of repentance and mourning over sin. As he saw God's heart reflected in the Scriptures, his own heart was moved. When he then read the Bible to the people, they joined him in this revival—and all it took was reading the

"Let the word of Christ richly dwell within you, with all wisdom teaching and admonishing one another with psalms and hymns and spiritual songs, singing with thankfulness in your hearts to God."

—The Apostle Paul Colossians 3:16

Word of God. No lengthy sermons were preached. No scholars tried to dissect each phrase. The Word was simply read, and it began to work.

Lest you think the experience of Josiah an isolated event, let me share with you another example of the power of reading the Word of God. In Nehemiah's day, too, God's Word had been neglected. But in Nehemiah 8, we learn that through the initiative of Ezra the Scriptures were read publicly to the people. They listened attentively, and the more they understood, the more it affected them. They shouted *"Amen, amen!"* and lifted their hands to the Lord (Nehemiah 8:6). Then they bowed low and worshiped the Lord with their faces to the ground in respect for His holiness. As they heard the neglected words of God, they began to weep (Nehemiah 8:9). But after their grieving came great joy and celebration as they understood what had been read. They even reinstated the observance of the feast of booths that had been neglected since the days of Joshua. They saw what God wanted, and they were moved to obey. The result was that *"there was great rejoicing"* (Nehemiah 8:17), and all of this happened because the Bible was read. You don't have to have a seminary degree to read your Bible. You just need to make time for it.

FOR ME TO FOLLOW GOD

Write down the main idea that spoke to you personally from today's lesson.

_____

_____

_____

_____

_____

_____

_____

_____

_____

_____

"I have rejoiced in the way of Your testimonies, as much as in all riches."

—Psalm 119:14

ACTS PRAYING

"A"—ADORATION—Take some time to praise God for who He is by identifying some of His attributes that you find particularly meaningful. Then express these attributes in a letter to Him. Take time to meditate on the passages quoted today.

_____

_____

_____

_____

_____

_____

_____

_____

"C"–CONFESSION—Remember, don't go looking for something to confess; instead, ask God to search your heart and bring to your mind anything that needs to be dealt with.

_____

_____

_____

_____

_____

_____

_____

_____

_____

"T"–THANKSGIVING—Thank God for the many blessings of your life, taking a moment to ask Him what you need to be thankful for.

_____

_____

_____

_____

_____

_____

_____

_____

_____

"S"–SUPPLICATION—Pray for God to work in your life, helping you to be faithful to His Word. Bring to Him any requests and needs that are on your heart, for yourself and others.

_____

_____

_____

_____

_____

_____

_____

_____

_____

"Open my eyes, that I may behold wonderful things from Your law."

—Psalm 119:18

Praying Scripture

You have ordained Your precepts, that we should keep them diligently. Oh that my ways may be established to keep Your statutes! Then I shall not be ashamed when I look upon all Your commandments. I shall give thanks to You with uprightness of heart, when I learn Your righteous judgments. (Psalm 119:4–7)

Main Point to Remember from Day Thirty:
Simply reading the Bible bears fruit in our lives.

Scripture ██ **DAY 31** ██

TAKING REFUGE IN THE WORD

We do not rely on any newly discovered law of science until it has been thoroughly tested and shown to be true. What a comfort it is to know that **every word of God has been tested in the crucible of human experience and proved to be true.** We read in Proverbs 30:5, *"Every word of God is tested; He is a shield to those who take refuge in Him."* The Hebrew word for "tested" has the idea of refined precious metal without any impurities (hence the King James Version translates it "pure"). The result to us is significant. Because every word of God has proved true, His promises provide a shield of protection and a place of refuge to us. Oh, the promises themselves aren't mystical, but as they show us truth about God, they show us how (and when) to take refuge in Him. Peter tells us in 2 Peter 1:4 that *"He has granted to us His precious and magnificent promises, so that by them you may become partakers of the divine nature."*

Our verse tells us *"He is a shield* **to those who take refuge in Him***"* (emphasis added). A shield is useless until you hide behind it. During the Vietnam War, flack jackets (bulletproof vests) were standard issue to most infantrymen. But because of the hot, humid, jungle conditions, they were often unworn, and many soldiers lost their lives because they weren't making use of the protection available to them. In the same way, the provision and protection of God's promises are of no benefit to us unless we take refuge in them, and we can't take refuge in them until we learn them and begin applying them. *"He is a shield to those who take refuge in Him."*

You and I need a steady diet of the Word of God. We need to be continually nourished by truth, and when our moment of need comes, we need to hold on to truth. When we find ourselves in crisis, we must stand on God's promises. It is difficult to stand on the promises of God if we have not made it a life habit to learn what they are and to trust them along the way. I find many believers don't really seek the Lord until something major happens in their lives. If we have not cultivated the habit of spending time with God when we are not in crisis, it will be unfamiliar territory when we are in crisis. Further, we miss the benefit of having truth already stored up for our time of need. Crisis ought to drive us to the Lord and make us cling more tightly to Him, but it shouldn't be the only time we speak with Him or listen to what He has to say to us.

As we are emphasizing all this week, one of the essential components of time with God is time in His Word—the Scriptures. Another essential that goes hand in hand with this is the principle of supplication—making our requests known through prayer. This is the real dynamic of communication with God.

> *"For by these He has granted to us His precious and magnificent promises, so that by them you may become partakers of the divine nature, having escaped the corruption that is in the world by lust."*
>
> **—Peter**
> **2 Peter 1:4**

It is a two-way street, talking to the Lord and letting Him speak to us as well. We all recognize prayer as important. But we often wrongly view prayer as simply us talking to God. What I want you to see today is that Scripture partners with prayer and in a sense is part of prayer as God speaks to us through His Word. True prayer is spirit to Spirit and involves listening as well as speaking. We want God to communicate with us. How does He do that? Do we hear an audible voice as John the Baptist did at Jesus' baptism or as Paul did on the Damascus road? Will we see a mysterious hand writing on the wall as King Belshazzar witnessed in Daniel's day? Certainly God is able to communicate with us however He chooses, but communication methods like the one described in Daniel is extremely rare. Most of what God has to say to us He says in the Bible. He spoke to Daniel of Israel's future when Daniel read the prophecies of Jeremiah. Jesus, being fully God, could have answered Satan's temptations in the wilderness however He chose, but He chose to answer with the Scriptures. The disciples recognized Jesus as Messiah because they knew the prophecies of Scripture. The people of Israel, in Ezra's day, ordered their lives in the right way because they read the Scriptures and God spoke to their hearts.

God's Word is not a dusty book of irrelevant words from the past. Hebrews 4:12 tells us, *"For the word of God is living and active and sharper than any two-edged sword, and piercing as far as the division of soul and spirit, of both joints and marrow, and able to judge the thoughts and intentions of the heart."* It is not simply a book that we read; it is a book that reads us. It speaks to our lives and our needs. What we learn from Proverbs 30:5 is the importance of how we respond when God speaks. *"Every word of God is tested. . . ."* It has already been proved true by others, and it offers a place of refuge for us. But each of us must read the Word and then take refuge in what it says. *"He is a shield to those who take refuge in Him."*

FOR ME TO FOLLOW GOD

What was the main point that you sensed God was speaking to you about as you considered the truths above?

_____

_____

_____

_____

ACTS PRAYING

"A"–ADORATION—Take a couple of minutes to focus on the greatness of God and to acknowledge Him for who He is. Meditate on Psalm 145:1–9, and write your observations in the space that follows.

_____

_____

_____

_____

_____

_____

_____

_____

"Give me understanding, that I may observe Your law and keep it with all my heart."

—Psalm 119:34

"C"–CONFESSION—As you are focusing on God, recite Psalm 139:23–24 as a prayer. If God brings any sins to your mind, confess them. However, don't dwell on these sins. Let God do the searching, not you.

_____

_____

_____

_____

_____

_____

_____

_____

"T"–THANKSGIVING—Take some time to thank God for the truth of Proverbs 30:5, for any other of His promises that come to mind, and for all the ways in which our lives are blessed. Express your thoughts in a prayer and write them here.

_____

_____

_____

_____

_____

_____

_____

_____

"Establish Your word to Your servant, as that which produces reverence for You."

—Psalm 119:38

"S"–SUPPLICATION—Pray for God's working in your life in showing you promises in which you need to take refuge.

_____

_____

_____

_____

_____

_____

_____

_____

Praying Scripture

Blessed are You, O Lord; teach me Your statutes. With my lips I have told of all the ordinances of Your mouth. I have rejoiced in the way of Your testimonies, as much as in all riches. I will meditate on Your precepts and regard Your ways. I shall delight in Your statutes; I shall not forget Your word. (Psalm 119:12–16)

Main Point to Remember from Day Thirty-One:
The promises of God's Word only benefit us when we take refuge in Him.

FAITH AND THE WORD

Psalm 46:10 makes an interesting and powerful statement: *"Cease striving and know that I am God; I will be exalted among the nations, I will be exalted in the earth."* In this verse we are told to *"cease striving,"* or, as the King James Version puts it, to *"be still."* The Hebrew word translated *"Cease striving"* basically means "to relax." Yet this message cannot be fully understood or appreciated until we understand its context. As we read Psalm 46, we discover that the author is facing some very difficult circumstances. The earth is changing. (The Hebrew word translated "change" in Scripture almost always has a negative connotation.) The waters are raging and overflowing. All around is catastrophe, yet the Lord's message in all of this is, *"Cease striving and know that I am God."*

What does this strange exhortation mean? The psalmist's world is falling apart; shouldn't he be trying to fix things, to minimize the damage? No. The most important thing to do when our world is falling apart is not to run around trying to put Band-Aids on everything, but to quit trusting our own efforts and focus our attention on God. He *"is our refuge and strength, a very present help in trouble"* (Psalm 46:1). What a difference it makes when we stop trying to solve all of our own problems and start trusting God! It is then and only then that we discover how great our God really is. It is as we *"cease striving"*—taking our focus off our circumstances and ourselves and placing it on our Lord—that we are able to face difficult times without being afraid.

How do we do this? How do we move from trial to trust? How do we draw our focus away from the problems that scream at us to the solution we have in God? How do we trust Him with the difficulties in our lives? Where does the faith we need come from? We will not be able to focus on God in our adversities and trust Him instead of ourselves without the Word. D. L. Moody said,

> *I prayed for faith and thought that some day faith would come down and strike me like lightening. But faith did not seem to come. One day I read in the tenth chapter of Romans, 'Now faith comes by hearing, and hearing by the Word of God.' I had closed my Bible and prayed for faith. I now opened my Bible and began to study and faith has been growing ever since.[2]*

A key component of our time with God must be time in His Word.

When my wife battled life-threatening cancer, it was the Word of God that got us through. Often I would sit by her hospital bed for hours reading Scripture out loud, for it would take hours of truth to move our focus from cancer to God. His Word became the liberation from our own striving.

> **"So faith comes from hearing, and hearing by the word of Christ."**
>
> **—The Apostle Paul
> Romans 10:17**

Time and time again, a particular Scripture would speak to our situation, giving us the comfort or guidance we needed.

God's words not only give us direction, they also give us the faith we need to face our difficulties. They reveal what He is able to do by showing us what He has done. When we see who He is and what He has accomplished for others, we are able to trust Him with our own trials. There is no faith without the Word of God.

FOR ME TO FOLLOW GOD

1. As you consider today's truth about the relationship between faith and the Word and the importance of trust, is there something in your present situation or in the days ahead to which it applies?

_____

_____

_____

_____

_____

_____

_____

2. Is there any situation in your past where it would have helped to apply this truth of trusting what God says?

_____

_____

_____

_____

_____

_____

_____

"This is my comfort in my affliction, that Your word has revived me."

—Psalm 119:50

ACTS PRAYING

"A"–ADORATION—Take some time to praise God for who He is by identifying some of His attributes that you find particularly meaningful. Then express these in a letter to Him. A good passage to meditate on today is Psalm 108.

_____

_____

_____

_____

_____

_____

"C"–CONFESSION—Remember, don't go looking for something to confess; instead, ask God to search your heart and bring to your mind anything that needs to be dealt with, especially in this area of trusting Him instead of your own efforts to solve life's problems.

_____

_____

_____

_____

_____

_____

_____

_____

"T"–THANKSGIVING—Thank God for the many blessings of your life, taking a moment to ask Him what you need to be thankful for. Thank God for His Word and its role in building your faith.

_____

_____

_____

_____

_____

_____

_____

_____

"S"–SUPPLICATION—Pray for God to work in your life, helping you to trust Him as difficult times come and to keep your focus on Him. If your present circumstances warrant it, pray through the trials you are going through right now, trusting them to God.

_____

_____

_____

_____

_____

_____

> *"You have dealt well with Your servant, O Lord, according to Your word."*
>
> *—Psalm 119:65*

My soul cleaves to the dust; revive me according to Your word. I have told of my ways, and You have answered me; teach me Your statutes. Make me understand the way of Your precepts, so I will meditate on Your wonders. My soul weeps because of grief; strengthen me according to Your word. Remove the false way from me, and graciously grant me Your law. (Psalm 119:25–29)

Main Point to Remember from Day Thirty-Two:
The Word of God builds our faith and helps us to trust Him.

Scripture **DAY 33**

LOOKING AT LIFE WITH A RENEWED MIND

One frustrating reality of living as a fallen creature in a fallen world is that bad things happen. Often life does not turn out the way that we desire. People hurt us; they let us down; they fail us. And we blow it, too. We make mistakes and wrong choices. But God looks at these things differently than we do. Perhaps one of the most comforting doctrines in all the Scriptures is the fact that God is sovereign. Because God is all-powerful and all-knowing, nothing that happens in our lives escapes His notice. And because He is sovereign, when bad things happen He takes notice and gets involved. More important, He uses these trials and difficulties for our good. In Romans 8:28–29 we read, *"And we know that God causes all things to work together for good to those who love God, to those who are called according to His purpose. For those whom He foreknew, He also predestined to become conformed to the image of His Son, so that He would be the firstborn among many brethren."* The promise of this passage—and I believe it is one of the greatest in Scripture—is that God is willing and able to take every negative situation in our lives and turn it around for our good. We may be tempted to say, "This situation I'm in sure doesn't look good to me!" This is because we see trials as bad. Note that the passage in Romans doesn't teach us that all things are good; it says that God is able to see the good in all things. Sin is still sin, and pain is still painful. The promise is not that we will avoid pain and difficulty, but that our all-loving, all-powerful Creator will turn the negatives around and cause them to work for our good.

Recognize that the good spoken of here is not the good of ease and comfort. Verse 29 makes it clear that God is working toward a much higher objective than simply making us feel good. His goal is to make us like Christ, and difficult circumstances are the tools of His trade. Consider Joseph, Jacob's son, as an example. His jealous brothers sold him into slavery, and then his boss's wife falsely accused him and threw him in prison. But God turned the situation around and used it to make Joseph prime minister over all of Egypt. When his brothers learned that he was alive, they feared for their lives, but Joseph told them, *"You meant evil against me, but God meant it for good"* (Genesis 50:20). Joseph recognized that God, who is sovereign, took their evil deed and caused something good to come out of it.

God is able to do the same in our lives if we will surrender our situations to Him. But there is one problem. When things get hard, we often do not look at our situations as God does. We try to interpret our difficulties with the

"You are good and do good; teach me Your statutes."

—Psalm 119:68

inadequate information of our limited perspective or through the fallen desires of our fleshly longing for the easy way out. We settle for the immediate cause (perhaps some evil done to us) instead of the ultimate purpose (God sovreignly allowing that evil because He can use it to bring about a good result in our lives and character.) We need to look higher than the immediate circumstance—high enough to see God and what He is doing through allowing the circumstances.

Later in Romans, Paul instructs us, *"Do not be conformed to this world, but be transformed by the renewing of your mind, so that you may prove what the will of God is, that which is good and acceptable and perfect"* (Romans 12:2). In the midst of trials, we are tempted to be like those of this world in our thinking. The whole fallen world system in which we live is continually trying to squeeze us into its mold and to get us to think in the same way as those who do not know God. To overcome this, I must experience the transforming work of God's Word renewing my mind. I must think as He does. It is only through understanding God's Word and obeying what it says that I am able to consistently choose to do God's will and to follow God's way. I am transformed as the Word changes my thinking.

The Greek word for "transformed" in Romans 12:2 (*metamorphoo*) is the origin of our English term "metamorphosis." It speaks of internal change. This is what God's Word does in us. Metamorphosis changes a tadpole so that it can climb out of the water and mud to a new world it didn't know before. Metamorphosis alters a caterpillar completely and enables it to fly into a new realm. A mind that is transformed by God's Word is likewise able to operate in a new realm. A frog can still live in the pond if it chooses, but it doesn't have to. A butterfly can still walk on land if it desires, but it now has the ability to fly above that realm as well. When God's Word renews our minds, we are transformed. We have new abilities that we did not possess before. Instead of avoiding trials, we are able to *"Count it all joy"* (James 1:2) when we encounter them, because we have God's perspective. We desperately need minds that have been reshaped by His Word to a right way of thinking.

FOR ME TO FOLLOW GOD

Write down the main idea that spoke to you personally from today's lesson.

_____

_____

_____

_____

ACTS PRAYING

"A"–ADORATION—Take some time to praise God for who He is, identifying some of His attributes that you find particularly meaningful and expressing these in your letter to Him. You may want to make use of a praise tape or some familiar choruses.

_____

_____

_____

_____

_____

"Forever, O Lord, Your word is settled in heaven."

—Psalm 119:89

"C"–CONFESSION—Don't look for something to confess; instead, ask God to search your heart and bring to your mind anything that needs to be dealt with, especially in this area of surrendering difficult situations to Him.

_____

_____

_____

_____

_____

_____

_____

_____

_____

"T"–THANKSGIVING—Thank God for the many blessings of your life, including His grace and work in and through you, and take a moment to ask God what you need to be thankful for.

_____

_____

_____

_____

_____

_____

_____

"If Your law had not been my delight, then I would have perished in my affliction."

—Psalm 119:92

"S"–SUPPLICATION—Pray for God to work in your life, renewing your mind to His way of thinking. Bring to Him any requests and needs that are on your heart.

_____

_____

_____

_____

_____

_____

_____

_____

Praying Scripture

Teach me, O Lord, the way of Your statutes, and I shall observe it to the end. Give me understanding, that I may observe Your law and keep it with all my heart. Make me walk in the path of Your commandments, for I delight in it. Incline my heart to Your testimonies and not to dishonest gain. Turn away my eyes from looking at vanity, and revive me in Your ways. Establish Your word to Your servant, as that which produces reverence for You. (Psalm 119:33–38)

Main Point to Remember from Day Thirty-Three:
Our minds must be reshaped by the Word so that we look at life as God does.

RECEIVING THE IMPLANTED WORD

Scripture **DAY 34**

In 1 Peter 2:1–3 we read, *"Therefore, putting aside all malice and all deceit and hypocrisy and envy and all slander, like newborn babies, long for the pure milk of the word, so that by it you may grow in respect to salvation, if you have tasted the kindness of the Lord."* Peter makes it clear that salvation is not simply the point of being forgiven for our sins. Once we taste of *"the kindness of the Lord,"* we must grow in our salvation. The Bible calls this process *"sanctification"*—salvation not just from the penalty of sin, but from its power as well, and this is a growth process. For a Christian, the Bible is just as important as milk is for a baby. Normally, one would not think of going without physical food for a week or even a day. No matter what stage of life we are in—baby or adult—physical food is necessary for physical growth and health. Without food, one eventually becomes weak and even ill. Lack of spiritual food has the same effect on our spiritual lives. Notice the progression Peter describes in how the Word helps us to grow. First, our hearts must be prepared for the Word. We must put aside those things that will make the Word unfruitful, such as malice, deceit, hypocrisy, envy, and slander. Then our hearts are ready to receive the Word.

How do we receive the Word of God into our hearts? When Jesus tells the parable of the sower in Matthew 13, He compares truth to a seed. The main point He is making is that the condition of the soil ultimately determines the fruit that grows. He relates,

> *Behold, the sower went out to sow; and as he sowed, some seeds fell beside the road, and the birds came and ate them up. Others fell on the rocky places, where they did not have much soil; and immediately they sprang up, because they had no depth of soil. But when the sun had risen, they were scorched; and because they had no root, they withered away. Others fell among the thorns, and the thorns came up and choked them out. And others fell on the good soil and yielded a crop, some a hundredfold, some sixty, and some thirty. (Matthew 13:3–8)*

This was not like the teaching the disciples were used to; it was simple and in terms they could grasp. It took what they already knew and helped them to understand what they didn't.

Jesus explained,

> *When anyone hears the word of the kingdom and does not understand it, the evil one comes and snatches away what has been sown in his heart. This is*

"Therefore, putting aside all filthiness and all that remains of wickedness, in humility receive the word implanted, which is able to save your souls."

—James
James 1:21

the one on whom seed was sown beside the road. The one on whom seed was sown on the rocky places, this is the man who hears the word and immediately receives it with joy; yet he has no firm root in himself, but is only temporary, and when affliction or persecution arises because of the word, immediately he falls away. And the one on whom seed was sown among the thorns, this is the man who hears the word, and the worry of the world and the deceitfulness of wealth choke the word, and it becomes unfruitful. And the one on whom seed was sown on the good soil, this is the man who hears the word and understands it; who indeed bears fruit and brings forth, some a hundredfold, some sixty, and some thirty. (Matthew 13:19–23)

What is the point of Jesus' parable? It is the condition of the soil, not the quality of the seed, that ultimately determines the fruit. Fortunately for us, the soil of our hearts is something we can plow and cultivate, just as ground is prepared for planting.

Jesus' brother, James, picks up on this analogy of the sower when he writes, *"Therefore putting aside all filthiness and all that remains of wickedness, in humility receive the word implanted, which is able to save your souls"* (James 1:21). In this verse, James concisely and with great clarity shows the operation of God's Word in the Christian life. To walk with Christ in a healthy way requires a putting off and a putting in. First, to make room for anything of value in our lives, we must sweep out all filthiness (specific acts of sin) and whatever remains of wickedness (the old, sinful nature). There must be a conscious and regular choice on our part to lay aside the old life, if the new one is to grow in a healthy way. Once we humble ourselves before God and do this, the soil of our hearts is ready for His Word to take root and bear fruit, the fruit of salvation.

When we speak of salvation, it is important to remember that salvation is a process and not merely a point. As W. E. Vine notes (in *The Expanded Vine's Expository Dictionary of New Testament Words,* Bethany House Publishers, 1984, p. 993), the Greek word used in James 1:21 for "save" speaks "of the present experiences of God's power to deliver from the bondage of sin." In other words, in the same way that the gospel planted in our hearts bears the fruit of justification, at every point of need for growth the solution is the same. Each of us must plant the specific truth of God's Word that relates to our individual needs in the fertile soil of a heart that is humble and cleansed of sin. Once the soil is prepared and the seed is planted, the result will be the fruit of changed character.

FOR ME TO FOLLOW GOD

1. As you consider today's truths concerning Scripture, is there some specific area you are aware of where you need to grow?

_____

_____

_____

_____

_____

_____

_____

_____

2. What truths from God's Word need to be implanted, related to the area just specified above?

_____

_____

_____

_____

_____

_____

_____

_____

_____

3. How well is the soil of your heart prepared for the seed of God's truth?

_____

_____

_____

_____

_____

_____

_____

_____

_____

"I will never forget Your precepts, for by them You have revived me."

—Psalm 119:93

ACTS PRAYING

"A"–ADORATION—Take some time to praise God for who He is by identifying some of His attributes that you find particularly meaningful. Then express these in your letter to Him. A good passage to meditate on today is Psalm 63.

_____

_____

_____

_____

_____

_____

_____

_____

_____

_____

"C"–CONFESSION—Don't go looking for something to confess; in faith, invite God to bring to your mind anything that needs to be dealt with, especially in light of the need to prepare the soil of your heart for the planting of His Word.

_____

_____

_____

_____

_____

_____

_____

_____

_____

"T"–THANKSGIVING—Thank God for the many blessings of your life, taking a moment to ask Him what you need to be thankful for.

_____

_____

_____

_____

_____

_____

_____

_____

_____

"S"–SUPPLICATION—Pray for God to work in your life, helping you to plant His Word in the areas where you need to grow. Pray for spiritual leaders in your life who sow the Word.

_____

_____

_____

_____

_____

_____

_____

_____

_____

"Your word is a lamp to my feet and a light to my path."

—Psalm 119:105

Praying Scripture

O how I love Your law! It is my meditation all the day. Your commandments make me wiser than my enemies, for they are ever mine. I have more insight than all my teachers, for Your testimonies are my meditation. I understand more than the aged, because I have observed Your precepts. . . . How sweet are Your words to my taste! Yes, sweeter than honey to my mouth! (Psalm 119:97–100, 103)

Main Point to Remember from Day Thirty-Four:
Each time a truth from God's Word takes root in our lives, it moves us further along in sanctification.

THE RIGHT APPROACH TO THE WORD OF GOD

Scripture **DAY 35**

Most of us as believers have access to plentiful servings of the Word of God. We can hear sermons and Sunday school lessons on Sunday; we can turn on a radio or television and listen to Bible teaching at any hour of the day. We can find Christian books on just about any subject. A number of cable television channels are devoted to preaching and teaching services. And beyond that, we can pick up the Word of God and read it for ourselves whenever we desire. But does this mean that we benefit from it? Not necessarily. Everyone who has these opportunities to be exposed to the Word isn't going to get the same blessing from them. Not all will get the same growth. Why? Because what we get out of the Word of God is determined by how we approach it, not just by the message itself. Two people hearing the same sermon may not both be blessed. Two Christians reading the same book are not guaranteed the same growth. It is how we approach the Word that shapes its work in us.

In Acts 17:11 we read, *"Now these* [the Bereans] *were more noble-minded than those in Thessalonica, for they received the Word with great eagerness, examining the Scriptures daily to see whether these things were so. Many of them therefore believed."* The message these Bereans received was from the apostle Paul, just as the epistles to the Thessalonians were. But Paul's divinely inspired message had a greater effect on the Bereans than on the Thessalonians. Certainly the Word of God has power to work, but the full effect of that work can be influenced by the way in which we receive it. The secret to the fruitful outcome of the Word's work in the Berean believers is in how they responded.

Three important things set the Bereans apart—made them *"more noble-minded."* First, they *"received the Word with great eagerness."* They were eager for the truth; they were teachable and wanted to learn. They didn't just want their ears tickled and their preconceptions supported; they wanted to hear from God. The seed of Scripture blooms when the soil is prepared to receive it. Second, they were *"examining the Scriptures daily to see whether these things were so."* They let the Bible, not other people, be their ultimate authority. This may not seem at first to be an essential requirement, but being teachable does not mean being gullible. Too many Christians only know what their pastors tell them of the Bible. They never check it out for themselves. As a result, they have beliefs but no convictions. Our confidence in something is based on our confidence in its source. We trust what we hear from preachers to the degree that we trust them. Sooner or later, that trust will be broken because all ministers—along with everyone else—are imperfect. But when

> **"Now these were more noble-minded than those in Thessalonica, for they received the word with great eagerness, examining the Scriptures daily to see whether these things were so."**
>
> **—Acts 17:11**

we take what we learn and confirm it with the whole counsel of Scripture, our confidence is no longer in the messenger but in God, the source of the message. It is then and only then that our beliefs become convictions with the strength to uphold us in the most challenging circumstances.

Finally, what set the Bereans apart was that they were willing to act on what they learned—at least, most of them were. The book of Acts tells us, *"Many of them therefore believed."* You see, unless we are willing to do something with what we learn, all the knowledge in the world does not benefit us. In fact, it can harm us. James 1:22 tells us, *"But prove yourselves doers of the word, and not merely hearers who delude themselves."* The Word benefits us when we are willing to obey what it says. If not, it becomes a deluding influence in our lives, deceiving us into thinking we are spiritual because of how much we know instead of how we live. Our objective ought to be to become Bereans—receiving the Word eagerly, investigating the Word carefully, and applying the Word willingly.

FOR ME TO FOLLOW GOD

Write down the main idea that spoke to you personally from today's lesson.

_____
_____
_____
_____
_____
_____
_____
_____
_____
_____
_____

ACTS PRAYING

"A"–ADORATION—Begin your time in prayer with praise to God for who He is, identifying some of His attributes that you find particularly meaningful and expressing these in your letter to Him.

_____
_____
_____
_____
_____
_____
_____
_____
_____
_____

"Your word is very pure, therefore Your servant loves it."

—Psalm 119:140

"C"–CONFESSION—Remember, don't go looking for something to confess; instead, ask God to search your heart and bring to your mind anything that needs to be dealt with.

_____
_____
_____
_____
_____
_____
_____
_____
_____

"T"–THANKSGIVING—Thank God for the many blessings of your life, taking a moment to ask Him what you need to be thankful for. Thank Him for His Word.

_____
_____
_____
_____
_____
_____
_____
_____
_____

"S"–SUPPLICATION—Pray for God to work in your life, helping you to grow in faithfulness to the Word. Bring to Him any requests and needs that are on your heart for yourself and others.

_____
_____
_____
_____
_____
_____
_____
_____

"The sum of Your word is truth, and every one of Your righteous ordinances is everlasting."

**—Psalm 119:160**

> *"I rejoice at Your word, as one who finds great spoil."*
>
> *—Psalm 119:162*

Praying Scripture

Let my cry come before You, O Lord; give me understanding according to Your word. Let my supplication come before You; deliver me according to Your word. Let my lips utter praise, for You teach me Your statutes. Let my tongue sing of Your word, for all Your commandments are righteousness. (Psalm 119:169–172)

Main Point to Remember from Day Thirty-Five:
It is how we approach the Word that shapes its work in us.

Main Ideas to Remember about the Principle of Scripture:
☐ God's Word performs a work in our lives when we believe.

☐ Simply reading the Bible bears fruit in our lives.

☐ The promises of God's Word only benefit us as we take refuge in Him.

☐ The Word of God builds our faith and helps us to trust Him.

☐ Our minds must be reshaped by the Word so that we look at life as God does.

☐ Each time a truth from God's Word takes root in our lives, it moves us further along in sanctification.

☐ It is how we approach the Word that shapes its work in us.

The Main Question to Ask Myself Is…
Am I letting the Word of God influence me?

Notes

1. As quoted by Pastor Steven J. Cole, October 3, 1993 in his sermon on "The Priority of God's Word" at Flagstaff Christian Fellowship.

2. From "Quotes by Famous Men," http://www.1Timothy4-13.com/files/chr_vik/quotes/.

The Principle of Supplication

Think about the last prayer meeting in which you participated. Wouldn't you say that what took place was basically a succession of requests to God? In our thoughts and actions, we live as if prayer equals asking. I'd like to challenge that notion, because it reflects an unhealthy view of prayer—one so narrow as to get in the way of effective praying. To turn prayer into an endless grocery list of requests is to miss the true definition of what prayer really is. True prayer is conversation with and communion with God. It is not simply talking **to** God, but rather, should be talking **with** God. It is a divine connection of your spirit with the Spirit of God. It should involve listening as well as speaking. And the speaking should be more than just reading requests. Where do you think your relationship with your wife or husband or best friend would be if your conversations were exclusively made up of asking? How do you think your parents would react if every time you spoke to them the gist of the discussion were "gimme, gimme, gimme"?

Before you draw the wrong conclusion about what I am saying, I need to qualify my message. I do not believe it is wrong to ask of God. In fact, we are invited to do so over and over again in the Bible. I am just saying is that asking is not all there is to prayer and that asking is not the right place to start. Therefore, I have placed the principle of supplication last among the principles of

"The prayer of the upright is His delight."

—Proverbs 15:8

time with God. In practice, this placement is essential. A lot of things ought to happen before we ask. This is far more than simple manners or spiritual etiquette; I believe that unless our asking is built on a firm foundation, it will not hold up. The first principle, our pursuit of God, affects our supplication, because it reveals that we want the Lord Himself, and not just what He gives. Adoration also shapes our what we ask of Him by causing our view of God to grow. Confession definitely influences our requests; the sure Word of God tells us, *"If I regard wickedness in my heart, the Lord will not hear"* (Psalm 66:18). Thanksgiving influences our asking in significant ways, because it reminds us of what God has already done and guards us from selfishness. Scripture molds our requests by models and by truth. A house built on such a sure foundation is sturdy indeed! If our hearts are right, God takes joy in our bringing requests to Him. *"The prayer of the upright is His delight"* (Proverbs 15:8).

THE FOUNDATION OF ASKING

Have you ever wondered what the secret to an effective prayer life is, or just what it would take to have your supplications answered? To most of us, the perfect, ideal plateau of spiritual communion with God seems elusive if not unattainable. In fact, if we're really honest, many of us have a warped appreciation for messages on prayer that make us feel bad about our lack of commitment to and perseverance in prayer. Somehow we feel as if we ought to feel bad. We don't expect to attain the ideal, so we see the next best thing as feeling bad about not reaching it. But that shouldn't be our focus at all. You see, a prayer life is not a tacked-on ritual that only the most devout add to their faith. An effective prayer life is the result of our relationship with God, not the reason for it. The secret is recognizing that it is the life that prays.

Let me explain what I mean by that. In James 5:16, we find one of the most quoted yet also most misunderstood passages on prayer in the New Testament: *"The effective prayer of a righteous man can accomplish much."* Most of us tend to place the emphasis of this verse on the words *"effective prayer,"* yet as we study this verse in its context, we find that the focus of the whole book is on being righteous (having genuine faith), not on effective prayer. The point is that the more godly and mature I become, the more effective my prayer life will be, because it is the life that prays. That is Jesus' point in John 15:7–8.

On the night of His betrayal, just before He would leave His disciples, Jesus instructed them, *"If you abide in Me, and My words abide in you, ask whatever you wish, and it will be done for you. My Father is glorified by this, that you bear much fruit, and so prove to be My disciples."* The promise of limitless answered prayer is the result first two conditions' having been met: (1) we are abiding in Him, and (2) His words are abiding in us. It doesn't take much reflection to understand why this is so. The more our relationship is built by abiding, the more in tune with His heart we become. The more His words abide in us, the more our asking is shaped by His truth and aligned with His will. We can ask whatever we wish because we wish for the same things that He does. This is a process, not a point, but the further we progress, the more effective our prayer life becomes. The results are exciting. As we abide in Him and His words abide in us (resulting in the renewal of our minds), we pray and God answers. This process of answered prayers has two additional

> *"If you abide in Me, and My words abide in you, ask whatever you wish, and it will be done for you."*
>
> —Jesus
> John 15:7

benefits: (a) God is glorified, and (b) we prove to all who see that we are His disciples. So if you want an effective prayer life, remember that it is the life that prays and focus on abiding in Him and in His Word.

FOR ME TO FOLLOW GOD
Write down the main idea that spoke to you personally from today's lesson.

_____

_____

_____

_____

_____

_____

_____

_____

_____

ACTS PRAYING

"A"–ADORATION—Take some time to praise God for who He is by identifying some of His attributes that you find particularly meaningful. Then express these in a letter to Him. You may want to make use of a praise tape or some familiar choruses.

_____

_____

_____

_____

_____

_____

_____

"C"–CONFESSION—Remember, don't go looking for something to confess; instead, ask God to search your heart and bring to your mind anything that needs to be dealt with, especially in this area of prayer and abiding in Him.

_____

_____

_____

_____

_____

_____

_____

_____

"Ask, and it will be given to you; seek, and you will find; knock, and it will be opened to you. For everyone who asks receives, and he who seeks finds, and to him who knocks it will be opened."

—Jesus
Matthew 7:7–8

"**What man is there among you who, when his son asks for a loaf, will give him a stone? Or if he asks for a fish, he will not give him a snake, will he? If you then, being evil, know how to give good gifts to your children, how much more will your Father who is in heaven give what is good to those who ask Him!**"

—Jesus
Matthew 7:9–11

"T"–THANKSGIVING—Thank God for the many blessings of your life, including His grace and His work in and through you. Also, take a moment to ask God what you need to be thankful for.

_____
_____
_____
_____
_____
_____
_____
_____
_____

"S"–SUPPLICATION—Pray for God to work in your life by showing you His will and helping you to do it. Bring to Him any requests and needs that are on your heart.

_____
_____
_____
_____
_____
_____
_____
_____
_____

Praying Scripture

> _Ah Lord God! Behold, You have made the heavens and the earth by Your great power and by Your outstretched arm! Nothing is too difficult for You (Jeremiah 32:17)._

Main Point to Remember from Day Thirty-Six:
Our asking is built on the foundation of abiding in Christ and allowing His Words to abide in us.

Supplication **DAY 37**

THE PRACTICE OF PRAYER

I have sought to be very cautious in explaining the title of today's study. When I speak of "the practice of prayer," I am not using the word "practice" like we would use it in say, the practice of medicine. The practice of prayer is not an activity reserved for professionals. I am talking about the actual doing of prayer. Any child of God can talk to the Father. You don't have to know how to speak King James English to talk with God. But it is helpful to understand how God wants us to talk with Him. A great passage to educate us on the proper practice of prayer is Philippians 4:6—*"Be anxious for nothing, but in everything by prayer and supplication with thanksgiving let your requests be made known to God."* Here we find specific directions on how to proceed in prayer. First, we must choose to lay aside our anxiety. Anxiety should always be seen as a red flag alerting us to the need to pray. Anxiety can simply mean that I appreciate the size of a challenge that is facing me. But anxiety or worry can be a direct result of trusting in myself and my own resources instead of in God. There are no guarantees that I will never feel anxious, and the feeling is not sin. But if I let anxiety or worry dictate my response to life and to God, that is sin, and it should be dealt with as such.

Worry can be a terrible taskmaster if I let it control me. But it can also be my servant, reminding me to cast my cares on the One who cares for me. The next thing we see in Philippians 4:6 is the boundaries of prayer. Paul says, *"in everything."* No matter how much we weasel and squirm, we cannot escape the reality that God wants us to talk with Him about everything, every area of our lives. Anything less is disobedience.

The next step in our process of prayer is to pray. This may sound silly, but the passage gives us specifics on how to go about this. First Paul says, *"in everything by prayer,"* which just means general prayer directed to God. We need to make sure that we are truly talking with God from our hearts. Next he says, *"and supplication."* This means to pray for particular benefits, in other words, to make our requests specific. If we don't learn to pray specifically, we'll never really know if our prayers are answered. We need to ask for things that are tangible and measurable. We are then told to accompany these requests *"with thanksgiving."* When we complete all three steps, we can make any request of God we desire—anything. Sound too good to be true? It is simply God's invitation to honesty. We are to bring our *"requests"* to Him; nothing is off-limits in prayer. We can ask God anything. I believe God is honored most by prayers that are "unspiritual" but honest. He wants us to bare our hearts to Him.

If we pray the right way, will God always give us what we request? Philippians 4:6 invites us to bring every request to God. We must notice, however, that God has not promised to always give us what we want. Sound unfair? Actually, what God promises is even better. *"And the peace of God, which surpasses all comprehension, will guard your hearts and your minds in Christ Jesus"* (Philippians 4:7). Instead of promising to honor all requests regardless of whether doing so would be beneficial to us or not, God promises to guard (literally, with a "garrison," or fortress) our hearts with His peace. If we have brought our desires to God in an honest manner, we can have confidence in the outcome. When we follow this very specific formula, we are in essence laying our requests at God's feet. Once we've done that, we can have confidence that He hears us. Psalm 4:3 reminds us, *"The Lord hears when I call to Him."* If God grants our requests, we can rejoice in His provision. If He chooses not to, we can trust that He knows what is best for us, and we can rejoice in His sovereignty. Either way, we win. Either way we can have peace, because our requests have now been filtered through God's will for us, which is good, acceptable, and perfect (Romans 12:2).

But what if God's will is not what I want? Ask yourself this: "Do I really want what my all-loving, all-knowing heavenly Father says is not best for me?" Are you willing to settle for something less than God's will?

> **"Be anxious for nothing, but in everything by prayer and supplication with thanksgiving let your requests be made known to God. And the peace of God, which surpasses all comprehension, will guard your hearts and your minds in Christ Jesus."**
>
> **—The Apostle Paul Philippians 4:6–7**

Write down the main idea that spoke to you personally from today's lesson.

_____

_____

_____

_____

_____

_____

_____

_____

_____

"Have faith in God. Truly I say to you, whoever says to this mountain, 'Be taken up and cast into the sea,' and does not doubt in his heart, but believes that what he says is going to happen, it will be granted him. Therefore I say to you, all things for which you pray and ask, believe that you have received them, and they will be granted you."

—Jesus
Mark 11:22–24

ACTS PRAYING

"A"–ADORATION—Take some time to praise God for who He is by identifying some of His attributes that you find particularly meaningful. Then express these in a letter to Him.

_____

_____

_____

_____

_____

_____

_____

"C"–CONFESSION—Don't go looking for something to confess; instead, ask God to search your heart and bring to your mind anything that needs to be dealt with.

_____

_____

_____

_____

_____

_____

_____

_____

_____

"T"–THANKSGIVING—Thank God for the many benefits of your walk with Him and for the joy of being able to pray honestly about anything. Take a moment to ask God what you need to be thankful for.

_____

_____

_____

_____

_____

_____

_____

_____

_____

_____

"S"–SUPPLICATION—Pray for God's wisdom in the choices of life, and ask Him to make you aware of others for whom you should be praying. Look for a specific way to apply today's principle in praying about something that is making you feel anxious.

_____

_____

_____

_____

_____

_____

_____

_____

_____

_____

_____

> *"Whatever you ask in My name, that will I do, so that the Father may be glorified in the Son. If you ask Me anything in My name, I will do it."*
>
> **—Jesus**
> **John 14:13–14**

Praying Scripture

Hear my prayer, O Lord! And let my cry for help come to You. Do not hide Your face from me in the day of my distress; incline Your ear to me; in the day when I call answer me quickly. (Psalm 102:1–2)

Main Point to Remember from Day Thirty-Seven:
We are free to bring any request to the Lord, and once it is in His hands, His peace will guard our hearts.

THE SIN OF NOT PRAYING FOR OTHERS

Supplication **DAY 38**

I f you have ever studied the Old Testament passages that tell the history of the kings of Israel, then you are already aware that the first king, Saul, was a failure. When the people of Israel demanded a king *"like all* the nations" (1 Samuel 8:5), they were rejecting God as their king and His leadership through the prophet Samuel (see 1 Samuel 8:7). One of the reasons Saul proved to be such a dismal failure was that God gave Israel exactly what the people requested so they could learn to want what He wanted for them. He would later bless them with David, a king after His heart. But though Samuel was no longer leader of Israel, in 1 Samuel 12:23–24 he assured them that he would still care for them and watch over them spiritually: *"Moreover, as for me, far be it from me that I should sin against the Lord by ceasing to pray for you; but I will instruct you in the good and right way. Only fear the Lord and serve Him in truth with all your heart; for consider what great things He has done for you."* Think of how he expresses his heart. Samuel considered it sin to ever stop praying for Israel. We often think of sin as something wrong that we do, but here Samuel defines sin as prayers left unsaid. Are we guilty of the sin of unsaid supplication?

Who are the VIPs in our lives that God would have us pray for? Obviously, we ought to be praying for those who are most important to us—our families and cherished friends. No one will pray as passionately for them as we would. But who else makes our prayer lists, and how long are those lists? Let's consider some of the people for whom Scripture tells us to pray. Obviously we see from Samuel's example that we must pray regularly for those under our spiritual charge. Maybe it is simply our children, whom we seek to bring up in the nurture and admonition of the Lord, or maybe our mates. We don't have to wait until we are married to pray for future spouses. Nor do we have to wait until we have children to begin praying for them. And no matter how long we have close family members, we shouldn't stop praying for them. Those involved in Bible study groups or Sunday School classes should pray for members of these groups, and we should all pray for our own churches (even if we aren't in charge of them). Over and over, Paul and other spiritual leaders said to their congregations, *"Pray for us"* (e.g., 1 Thessalonians 5:25, 2 Thessalonians 3:1, and Hebrews 13:18). We have a responsibility to pray for those who lead us spiritually as well as those whom we lead.

Scripture is not silent on instructions concerning those for whom we need to pray. In Psalm 122:6 we read, *"Pray for the peace of Jerusalem."* God's people, Israel, need our prayers, but so too do those who inhabit our own Jerusalems—the communities in which we live. Paul wrote to Timothy, *"First of all, then, I urge that entreaties and prayers, petitions and thanksgivings, be made on behalf of all men, for kings and all who are in authority, so that we may lead a tranquil and quiet life in all godliness and dignity"* (1 Timothy 2:1–2). All of the authorities in our lives need our prayers, and we are commanded to pray for them. If we want right and godly government, it comes not just by voting, but by what is even more important, by kneeling in prayer. What prayers do we pray for those who govern us? Obviously, they need wisdom to lead,; hearts inclined to justice and fairness, and discernment in decisions. But that is not all. Paul goes on to say that, when we pray for our leaders, it *"is good and acceptable in the sight of God our Savior, who desires all men to be saved and to come to the knowledge of the truth"* (1 Timothy 2:3–4). Most of all we should pray for their salvation.

Through the gift of supplication, we can enter into the needs of others. We can travel great distances on our knees. The book of James teaches us that one focus of our petitions should be those who are sick, stating that *"the prayer offered in faith will restore the one who is sick. . . . Therefore . . . pray for one another so that you may be healed"* (James 5:15–16). But that is not the only need I can come along side. Ephesians 6:18 exhorts us, *"With all prayer and*

> *"Moreover, as for me, far be it from me that I should sin against the Lord by ceasing to pray for you; but I will instruct you in the good and right way. Only fear the Lord and serve Him in truth with all your heart; for consider what great things He has done for you."*
>
> **—Samuel**
> **1 Samuel 12:23–24**

petition pray at all times in the Spirit, and with this in view, be on the alert with all perseverance and petition for all the saints." The context there is spiritual warfare, and certainly we need to be praying for our brothers and sisters who are under the attack of the enemy through trials or temptations. Paul goes on to ask members of the church at Ephesus, *"Pray on my behalf, that utterance may be given to me in the opening of my mouth, to make known with boldness the mystery of the gospel"* (Ephesians 6:19). We certainly need to pray for those who take the gospel to unbelievers.

There is one other category I would like to mention as we consider who needs our prayers. We must pray for those we don't want to pray for. In the Sermon on the Mount, Jesus said, *"But I say to you, love your enemies and pray for those who persecute you"* (Matthew 5:44). Through prayer, we can work to turn enemies into friends. Our supplication matters. We may not always see the difference, but it always makes a difference. Revelation 5:8 speaks of *"golden bowls full of incense, which are the prayers of the saints."* These are kept in the presence of the Lord in heaven. That idea ought to motivate us to avoid the sin of unsaid supplication.

FOR ME TO FOLLOW GOD

Write down the main idea that spoke to you personally from today's lesson.

_____
_____
_____
_____
_____
_____
_____
_____
_____

ACTS PRAYING

"A"–ADORATION—Take some time to praise God for who He is by identifying some of His attributes that you find particularly meaningful. Then express these in a letter to Him.

_____
_____
_____
_____
_____
_____
_____
_____
_____
_____
_____

> *"Truly, truly, I say to you, if you ask the Father for anything in My name, He will give it to you. Until now you have asked for nothing in My name; ask, and you will receive, so that your joy may be made full.*
>
> **—Jesus**
> **John 16:23–24**

"C"–CONFESSION—Remember, don't go looking for something to confess; instead, ask God to search your heart and bring to your mind anything that needs to be dealt with especially in the area of neglected prayer.

_____

_____

_____

_____

_____

_____

_____

_____

_____

_____

_____

"T"–THANKSGIVING—Thank God for the many blessings of your life, taking a moment to ask Him for what (and for whom) you need to be thankful.

_____

_____

_____

_____

_____

_____

_____

_____

_____

_____

"This is the confidence which we have before Him, that, if we ask anything according to His will, He hears us. And if we know that He hears us in whatever we ask, we know that we have the requests which we have asked from Him."

—The Apostle John
1 John 5:14–15

"S"–SUPPLICATION—Put into practice what you learned today about those for whom you need to pray.

_____

_____

_____

_____

_____

_____

_____

_____

_____

_____

Praying Scripture

This is what Jesus prayed for His disciples:

I ask on their behalf . . . for they are Yours. . . . Holy Father, keep them in Your name, the name which You have given Me, that they may be one even as We are. . . . I do not ask You to take them out of the world, but to keep them from the evil one. . . . Sanctify them in the truth; Your word is truth. (John 17:9, 11, 15, 17)

Main Point to Remember from Day Thirty-Eight:

We have a responsibility to pray for others, and it is a sin not to do that.

THE MODEL FOR PRAYER

Supplication DAY 39

Within the circles of Christendom, some very different ideas exist concerning how we are to approach God with our requests. I believe that we cannot consider the principle of supplication without addressing some that I consider to be wrong. I group them with personalities. First, there is what I call "brat" praying. Sometimes I hear people approach God as a spoiled child would his parents, with a selfish attitude of "I want!" Then there is what I call "beggar" praying. This approach to God doesn't even acknowledge that He has called us His children. It is prayer that asks for requests based only on His mercy, but it is also prayer that tries to wear God down. It keeps begging the same requests over and over in the hope that, if only from a desire to silence the prayers, God will grant the petitioners what they ask. One of the most offensive types of prayer to me (and perhaps to God) is what I call "boss" praying. Sometimes in prayer gatherings I hear people talk to God as if they are His boss, as they command Him what to do. They treat Scriptural principles as a legal brief they can use against God to force Him to deliver what they want, when they want it. Although I have faith in all of the promises of God, I want to make sure I interpret them correctly and leave the decision with Him in how and when to fulfill them. I believe that these approaches—the brat, the beggar, and the boss— are neither right nor biblical.

So how do we make requests of God? What is the right process for petition? When the disciples discussed this with Jesus, He gave them what we call the Lord's Prayer:

Our Father who is in heaven, hallowed be Your name. Your kingdom come. Your will be done, on earth as it is in heaven. Give us this day our daily bread. And forgive us our debts, as we also have forgiven our debtors. And do not lead us into temptation, but deliver us from evil. (For Yours is the kingdom and the power and the glory forever. Amen.) (Matthew 6:9–13)

It was not given as a mystical prayer, but rather as a model. Verse 9 begins, *"Pray then in this way. . . . "* Each phrase represents a principle of how we are to approach the Father. And though I think it is worthwhile to meditate on each phrase, in this lesson I'd like to simply highlight a few that relate to supplication.

When Jesus invites me to pray, *"Our Father,"* it ought to remind me that my good is not the only good, because my God is not only mine. Is it right for me to pray for my side to win a game or a war when believers on the other side pray to the same God? *"Our Father"* also reminds me that my prayer to God is affected by my relationship with His children (see Matthew 6:14). The

"Your Father knows what you need before you ask Him."

**—Jesus
Matthew 6:8**

phrase *"who is in heaven"* reminds me that God is in heaven and I am not. He can see what I cannot see, and He thinks not temporally but eternally, whereas many of my requests are for temporal, short-term good that may not be best in an eternal sense. I want ease and comfort even at the expense of growth and benefit to others. Just before teaching the disciples how to pray, Jesus had addressed how not to pray. He told them not to pray like hypocritical Pharisees, trying to sound pious to men rather than addressing their prayer to God (Matthew 6:5). He told them not to pray like Gentiles, who trusted in mystical words and multiplied prayers to be heard (Matthew 6:7). He reminded them, *"your Father knows what you need before you ask Him"* (Matthew 6:8).

Perhaps the most important principle of supplication we find is in the phrase, *"hallowed be Your name."* Our petition must be painted with reverence. We need a lofty view of the Person to whom we are talking as we make our requests. Although the word *"Father"* speaks of intimacy, we cannot let that lead to such familiarity that we lose our reverence for Him. It isn't noticeable when we read our English Bible, but two different Greek words are both translated "ask" in the New Testament. One word (*erotao*) is used to speak of a petition that would be made to a peer. It means asking of an equal. Although this word is used almost sixty times in the New Testament, it is **never** used for a believer asking something of God! Another Greek word (*aiteo*) conveys a very different meaning. It refers to a request of a superior made by an inferior. It is used over seventy times in the New Testament. This is the Greek word used in Matthew 7:9 when Jesus says, *"What man is there among you who, when his son asks for a loaf, will give him a stone?"* We have the freedom of a child to make requests of our Father, but we need to recognize that we are not his equals. Only Jesus is that kind of Son.

In John 14, we see both Greek words for "ask" in use. In John 14:14, Jesus says, *"If you ask [aiteo] Me anything in My name, I will do it."* In John 14:16 Jesus says, *"I will ask [erotao] the Father. . . ."* Only He can ask anything of God as an equal. As we bring our petitions to the Lord, we are invited to ask, but in our asking we must make sure that His name is *"hallowed."*

FOR ME TO FOLLOW GOD

Write down the main idea that spoke to you personally from today's lesson.

_____

_____

_____

_____

_____

_____

_____

_____

_____

_____

ACTS PRAYING

"A"–ADORATION—Take some time to praise God for who He is by identifying some of His attributes that you find particularly meaningful. Then express these in a letter to Him.

> "Now to Him who is able to do far more abundantly beyond all that we ask or think, according to the power that works within us, to Him be the glory in the church and in Christ Jesus to all generations forever and ever. Amen."
>
> —The Apostle Paul
> Ephesians 3:20–21

_____

_____

_____

_____

_____

_____

_____

_____

_____

"C"–CONFESSION—Remember, don't go looking for something to confess; instead, ask God to search your heart and bring to your mind anything that needs to be dealt with.

_____

_____

_____

_____

_____

_____

_____

_____

_____

_____

"T"–THANKSGIVING—Thank God for the many blessings of your life, taking a moment to ask Him what you need to be thankful for.

_____

_____

_____

_____

_____

_____

_____

_____

_____

"S"–SUPPLICATION—Bring your requests to God, your Father, with an attitude of reverence that hallows His name.

_____
_____
_____
_____
_____
_____
_____
_____
_____

Praying Scripture

Our Father who is in heaven, hallowed be Your name. Your kingdom come. Your will be done, on earth as it is in heaven. Give us this day our daily bread. And forgive us our debts, as we also have forgiven our debtors. And do not lead us into temptation, but deliver us from evil. (For Yours is the kingdom and the power and the glory forever. Amen.) (Matthew 6:9–13)

Main Point to Remember from Day Thirty-Nine:

As we make requests of God, it must be with reverence toward Him, as inferiors asking something of a superior.

> "The effective prayer of a righteous man can accomplish much."
>
> **—James**
> **James 5:16**

Supplication **DAY 40**

ADVICE FROM A PRAYER WARRIOR

The term "prayer warrior" is an interesting one, for it conveys the accurate idea that in the spiritual realm we can wage war on our knees. Prayer gives us the ability to transcend space and time. We can instantly travel to the far side of the world to labor with a missionary. We can even cross time and move into the future with our requests. Prayer does not know the same boundaries that govern other physical activities. As we close our consideration of supplication and the role it plays in our time with God, I thought it useful to offer the advice of an expert. I don't mean me, because I don't place myself in that category. Rather, I want to bring to you some inspired words from the pages of Scripture, spoken by one of the early church fathers. He earned the nickname "Camel Knees" because his extreme devotion to prayer calloused his knees with wrinkles resembling those of a camel. He was James, our Lord's brother, and he wrote the book of the Bible that bears his name.

One would expect that if someone nicknamed Camel Knees wrote a book, it would be about prayer. Yet as you read the book of James, the subject is conspicuous by its near absence. Instead, James focuses on being a righteous person, someone with an authentic faith. When he says at the end of the book, *"The effective prayer of a righteous man can accomplish much"* (James 5:16), he puts the focus not on having effective prayer but on being righteous. His point seems to be that, if you become righteous, your prayers **will** be effective. Often we try to become godly by praying more, rather than realizing that this is putting the cart before the horse. My prayer life will never go any further than my walk with God. The godlier we become, the more effective our praying will be. What does your prayer life say about the progress of your spiritual maturity? If your prayer life isn't what it ought to be, you won't change it by trying harder to pray. You will only change it as you grow in a real faith relationship with Christ, and that begins with surrender—becoming a *"bondservant"* as James did. He surrendered his life to God as his Master, committing to do only His will.

James does make a handful of references to prayer in his book, and each is significant. In the context of trials he advises, *"If any of you lacks wisdom, let him ask of God, who gives to all generously and without reproach, and it will be given to him. But he must ask in faith without any doubting"* (James 1:5–6). When we need wisdom, we can ask God, and He will give it without resenting the request. But we must ask in faith that takes Him at His word. This means trusting that He will answer and waiting patiently until He does. In chapter 4, James brings up prayer again when he states, *"You do not have because you do not ask. You ask and do not receive, because you ask with wrong motives, so that you may spend it on your pleasures"* (James 4:2–3). One of our problems in prayer is that we strive for what we want instead of taking those desires to the Lord. We ought to be trusting God with those desires and allowing Him to veto if He knows what we want will not be good for us. Perhaps that is the very reason we don't ask God—we are afraid of how He will answer. We ought to be taking every desire to Him in prayer. Instead, we envy and quarrel and fight as we strive for what we want. It may very well be that the reason we don't always ask everything of God is that often we aren't sure we want to know His answer. If the only motive of the request is selfish pleasure, we probably already know in our hearts that God is going to say no. Instead of risking that, we take matters into our own hands. James makes clear that one of the reasons prayers go unanswered is that the motives behind them are wrong. But if we really love the Lord, we ought to bring every request to Him—not so that we can get what we want, but so that we can get what He wants us to have.

At the end of the book of James, we gain one last rich perspective on prayer. After telling us that *"the effective prayer of a righteous man can accomplish much"* (James 5:16), he helps us understand what that means with an example. He makes reference to two powerful prayers the prophet Elijah prayed. First, Elijah *"prayed earnestly that it would not rain, and it did not rain on the earth for three years and six months"* (James 5:17). Though we are not told when or why Elijah prayed this, what characterized his ministry was the phrase *"the word of the Lord"* (1 Kings 18:1). He would hear from God and then act. I do not believe that he came up with an idea and then asked God to bless it. Instead, he asked God to do what God had already told him He was going to do. This is clear from James's second example: *"He prayed again, and the sky poured rain and the earth produced its fruit"* (James 5:18). Elijah prayed for rain in 1 Kings 18:42–45, but in 1 Kings 18:1 God had already told him He was going to send rain. What is effective prayer? It is prayer that takes God at His Word and asks Him to do what He has already revealed as His will. One of the most powerful ways to pray is to pray Scripture—what God has already said. Effective prayer is not our coming up with an idea and asking God to fulfill it, but our trusting God to do what He has said he will do. It is praying as a *"righteous"* person (one in right relationship to God), and it is prayer aligned with His will. That is what our supplication ought always be.

> **"But if any of you lacks wisdom, let him ask of God, who gives to all generously and without reproach, and it will be given to him. But he must ask in faith without any doubting, for the one who doubts is like the surf of the sea, driven and tossed by the wind."**
>
> **—James**
> **James 1:5–6**

> **"You do not have because you do not ask. You ask and do not receive, because you ask with wrong motives, so that you may spend it on your pleasures."**
>
> **—James**
> **James 4:2–3**

FOR ME TO FOLLOW GOD

Write down the main idea that spoke to you personally from today's lesson.

_____

_____

_____

_____

_____

_____

_____

_____

ACTS PRAYING

"A"–ADORATION—Take some time to praise God for who He is by identifying some of His attributes that you find particularly meaningful. Then express these in a letter to Him.

_____

_____

_____

_____

_____

_____

_____

_____

"C"–CONFESSION—Ask God to search your heart and to bring to mind anything that needs to be dealt with. Consider whether you have been asking with motives that are wrong (selfish).

_____

_____

_____

_____

_____

_____

_____

_____

_____

"T"–THANKSGIVING—Thank God for the many benefits of your walk with Him and for the joy of being able to ask Him about anything. Take a moment to ask Him what you need to be thankful for.

_____

_____

_____

_____

_____

_____

_____

_____

"S"–SUPPLICATION—Pray for God's wisdom in the choices of life, and ask Him to make you aware of others for whom you should be praying.

_____

_____

_____

_____

_____

_____

_____

Praying Scripture

Now to [You] who [are] able to keep [us] from stumbling, and to make [us] stand in the presence of [Your] glory blameless with great joy, to the only God our Savior, through Jesus Christ our Lord, be glory, majesty, dominion and authority, before all time and now and forever. Amen. (Jude 1:24–25)

Main Point to Remember from Day Forty:

We must be sure that we ask in faith, with hearts that are right and with right motives.

Main Ideas to Remember about the Principle of Scripture:

❏ Our asking is built on the foundation of abiding in Christ and allowing His Words to abide in us.

❏ We are free to bring any request to the Lord, and once it is in His hands, His peace will guard our hearts.

❏ We have a responsibility to pray for others, and it is a sin not to do that.

❏ As we make requests of God, it must be with reverence toward Him, as inferiors asking of a superior.

❏ We must be sure that we ask in faith, with hearts that are right and with right motives.

The Main Question to Ask Is . . .

Am I asking of God correctly?

> **"Is anyone among you sick? Then he must call for the elders of the church and they are to pray over him, anointing him with oil in the name of the Lord; and the prayer offered in faith will restore the one who is sick, and the Lord will raise him up, and if he has committed sins, they will be forgiven him."**
>
> **—James**
> **James 5:14–15**

How to Follow God

STARTING THE JOURNEY

Did you know that you have been on God's heart and mind for a long, long time? Even before time existed you were on His mind. He has always wanted you to know Him in a personal, purposeful relationship. He has a purpose for your life and it is founded upon His great love for you. You can be assured it is a good purpose and it lasts forever. Our time on this earth is only the beginning. God has a grand design that goes back into eternity past and reaches into eternity future. What is that design?

The Scriptures are clear about God's design for man—God created man to live and walk in oneness with Himself. Oneness with God means being in a relationship that is totally unselfish, totally satisfying, totally secure, righteous and pure in every way. That's what we were created for. If we walked in that kind of relationship with God we would glorify Him and bring pleasure to Him. Life would be right! Man was meant to live that way—pleasing to God and glorifying Him (giving a true estimate of who God is). Adam sinned and shattered his oneness with God. Ever since, man has come short of the glory of God: man does not and cannot please God or give a true estimate of God. Life is not right until a person is right with God. That is very clear as we look at the many people who walked across the pages of Scripture, both Old and New Testaments.

JESUS CHRIST came as the solution for this dilemma. Jesus Christ is the glory of God—the true estimate of who God is in every way. He pleased His Father in everything He did and said, and He came to restore oneness with God. He came to give man His power and grace to walk in oneness with God, to follow Him day by day enjoying the relationship for which he was created. In the process, man could begin to present a true picture of Who God is and experience knowing Him personally. You may be asking, "How do these facts impact my life today? How does this become real to me now? How can I begin the journey of following God in this way?" To come to know God personally means you must choose to receive Jesus Christ as your personal Savior and Lord.

- First of all, you must admit that you have sinned, that you are not walking in oneness with God, not pleasing Him or glorifying Him in your life (Romans 3:23; 6:23; 8:5-8).
- It means repenting of that sin—changing your mind, turning to God and turning away from sin—and by faith receiving His forgiveness based on His death on the Cross for you (Romans 3:21-26; 1 Peter 3:18).
- It means opening your life to receive Him as your living, resurrected Lord and Savior (John 1:12). He has promised to come and indwell you by His Spirit and live in you as the Savior and Master of your life (John 14:16-21; Romans 14:7-9).
- He wants to live His life through you—conforming you to His image, bearing His fruit through you and giving you power to reign in life (John 15:1,4-8; Romans 5:17; 7:4; 8:29, 37).

You can come to Him now. In your own words, simply tell Him you want to know Him personally and you willingly repent of your sin and receive His forgiveness and His life. Tell Him you want to follow Him forever (Romans 10:9-10, 13). Welcome to the Family of God and to the greatest journey of all!!!

WALKING ON THE JOURNEY

How do we follow Him day by day? Remember, Christ has given those who believe in Him everything pertaining to life and godliness, so that we no longer have to be slaves to our "flesh" and its corruption (2 Peter 1:3-4). Day by day He wants to empower us to live a life of love and joy, pleasing to Him and rewarding to us. That's why Ephesians 5:18 tells us to *be filled with the Spirit*—keep on being controlled by the Spirit who lives in you. He knows exactly what we need each day and we can trust Him to lead us (Proverbs 3:5-6). So how can we cooperate with Him in this journey together?

To walk with Him *day by day* means ...
- reading and listening to His Word day by day (Luke 10:39, 42; Colossians 3:16; Psalm 19:7-14; 119:9).
- spending time talking to Him in prayer (Philippians 4:6-7).
- realizing that God is God and you are not, and the role that means He has in your life.

This allows Him to work through your life as you fellowship, worship, pray and learn with other believers (Acts 2:42), and serve in the good works He has prepared for us to do—telling others who Jesus is and what His Word says, teaching and encouraging others, giving to help meet needs, helping others, etc. (Ephesians 2:10).

God's goal for each of us is that we be conformed to the image of His Son, Jesus Christ (Romans 8:29). But none of us will reach that goal of perfection until we are with Him in Heaven, for then "we shall be like Him, because we shall see Him just as He is" (1 John 3:2). For now, He wants us to follow

Him faithfully, learning more each day. Every turn in the road, every trial and every blessing, is designed to bring us to a new depth of surrender to the Lord and His ways. He not only wants us to do His will, He desires that we surrender to His will His way. That takes trust—trust in His character, His plan and His goals (Proverbs 3:5-6).

As you continue this journey, and perhaps you've been following Him for a while, you must continue to listen carefully and follow closely. We never graduate from that. That sensitivity to God takes moment by moment surrender, dying to the impulses of our flesh to go our own way, saying no to the temptations of Satan to doubt God and His Word, and refusing the lures of the world to be unfaithful to the Lord who gave His life for us.

God desires that each of us come to maturity as sons and daughters: to that point where we are fully satisfied in Him and His ways, fully secure in His sovereign love, and walking in the full measure of His purity and holiness. If we are to clearly present the image of Christ for all to see, it will take daily surrender and daily seeking to follow Him wherever He leads, however He gets there (Luke 9:23-25). It's a faithful walk of trust through time into eternity. And it is worth everything. Trust Him. Listen carefully. Follow closely.

The *Following God*
Bible Character Study Series

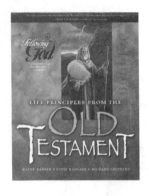

Life Principles from the Old Testament

Characters include: Adam, Noah, Job, Abraham, Lot, Jacob, Joseph, Moses, Caleb, Joshua, Gideon, and Samson
ISBN 0-89957-300-2   208 pages

Life Principles from the Kings of the Old Testament

Characters include: Saul, David, Solomon, Jereboam I, Asa, Ahab, Jehoshaphat, Hezekiah, Josiah, Zerubbabel & Ezra, Nehemiah, and "The True King in Israel."
ISBN 0-89957-301-0   256 pages

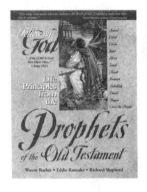

Life Principles from the Prophets of the Old Testament

Characters include: Samuel, Elijah, Elisha, Jonah, Hosea, Isaiah, Micah, Jeremiah, Habakkuk, Daniel, Haggai, and "Christ the Prophet."
ISBN 0-89957-303-7   224 pages

Leader's Guides for Following God™ books are available.
To order now, call (800) 266-4977 or (423) 894-6060.
Or order online at www.amgpublishers.com

The *Following God*
Bible Character Study Series

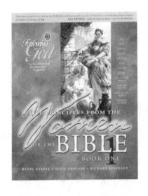

Life Principles from the Women of the Bible (Book One)

Characters include: Eve, Sarah, Miriam, Rahab, Deborah, Ruth, Hannah, Esther, The Virtuous Woman, Mary & Martha, Mary, the Mother of Jesus, and "The Bride of Christ."
ISBN 0-89957-302-9   224 pages

Life Principles from the Women of the Bible (Book Two)

Characters include: Hagar, Lot's Wife, Rebekah, Leah, Rachel, Abigail, Bathsheba, Jezebel, Elizabeth, The Woman at the Well, Women of the Gospels, and "The Submissive Wife."
ISBN 0-89957-308-8   224 pages

Life Principles from the New Testament Men of Faith

Characters include: John the Baptist, Peter, John, Thomas, James, Barnabas, Paul, Paul's Companions, Timothy, and "The Son of Man."
ISBN 0-89957-304-5   208 pages

Call for more information (800) 266-4977 or (423) 894-6060.
Or order online at www.amgpublishers.com

Following God™ Discipleship Series

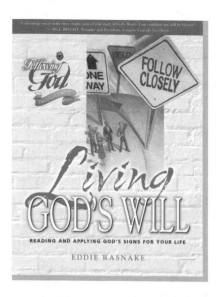

Living God's Will

ISBN 0-89957-309-6

How can I follow and identify the signs that lead to God's will? *Living God's Will* explores the answer to this all-important question in detail. It is Eddie Rasnake's deeply-held conviction that the road to God's will is well-marked with signposts to direct us. Each lesson in this twelve-week Bible study takes a look at a different signpost that reflects God's will. You will be challenged to recognize the signposts of God when you encounter them. But more importantly, you will be challenged to follow God's leading by following the direction of those signposts.

In the pages of this "Following God" study on finding and obeying God's will, you will find clear and practical advice for:

✓ Yielding your life to the Lord

✓ Recognizing God's will through Scripture, prayer and circumstances

✓ Seeking godly counsel

✓ Discovering how God's peace enters into the process of following His will

✓ Determining God's will in areas not specifically addressed in Scripture, such as choosing a wife/husband or career path.

Throughout your study you will also be enriched by the many interactive application sections that literally thousands have come to appreciate from the acclaimed **Following God** series.

To order, call (800) 266-4977 or (423) 894-6060
www.amgpublishers.com

Other Discipleship Series books now available.
Watch for new Following God™ titles to be released soon!

Following God™ Discipleship Series

First Steps for the New Christian

ISBN 0-89957-311-8

I'm new to this. I didn't even know I was in a race. The Bible likens the Christian life to a marathon. The apostle Paul said, *Run in such a way that you may win."* **Following God™—** *First Steps for the New Christian* will help you start out on the right foot and stay there with practical studies designed to get new runners in shape to finish the race.

In the pages of this book, you will find clear and practical advice that answers the following questions:

- ✓ What is your position in Christ?
- ✓ What is spiritual growth and what is not spiritual growth?
- ✓ How should a Christian deal with sin?
- ✓ How important are Bible study, prayer, and meditation to the Christian walk?
- ✓ What should Christians do to cultivate the gifts, talents, and opportunites that God gives them?

Throughout your study you will also be enriched by the many interactive application sections that literally thousands have come to appreciate from the acclaimed **Following God** series.

To order, call (800) 266-4977 or (423) 894-6060
www.amgpublishers.com

Other Discipleship Series books now available.
Watch for new Following God™ titles to be released soon!

Keith
Urban
Be Here

Brad Paisley.
Time Well Wasted.

CD's Michelle Mackenzie